TOTALLY
SURRENDERED
AND COMPLETELY
HIS

—————— Dianna DeYoung ——————

ISBN 978-1-63814-060-3 (Paperback)
ISBN 978-1-63814-061-0 (Digital)

Unless otherwise noted, all scripture quotations are from the New American Standard Bible (NASB). New American Standard Bible Copyright (c) 1960, 1962, 1963, 1968, 1971, 1972, 1973, 1975, 1977, 1995 by The Lockman Foundation, La Habra, California. All rights reserved http://www.lockman.org. Used by Permission.

Mack Brock. "Greater Things." Greater Things, Sparrow 2018. Audio CD. Accessed 2018 via radio station.

All names have been changed to protect.

Covenant Books, Inc.
11661 Hwy 707
Murrells Inlet, SC 29576
www.covenantbooks.com

This book is dedicated to my sons.

Contents

Introduction

I wrote this book out of obedience. I heard the Father's voice over and over again saying to me, "Write the book." When it first started, I would brush it off. I wasn't sure if it was even Him telling me to do it, and furthermore, I had no idea how to do it.

One Sunday while in church, someone I knew well came up to me and said, "I have a word for you. The Lord has asked you to do something and it will take you out of your comfort zone and you don't want to do it." That day, I started writing the book.

I have so many experiences of His goodness and faithfulness to me. How could I not tell? How could I be silent?

Everyone has a past. Without the past, I wouldn't have a story. I am grateful and thankful for my past and the person I am today because of it—a better person. The horrible and evil things that we go through do not define us. It's not our identity. It's just a chapter in our story.

I have dedicated this book to my sons. I want to leave a legacy of hearing His voice, obeying and experiencing the miracles that follow! Even in the midst of my weaknesses and failures, my sons will see that He is still good and faithful.

It is important to me that as you read this book, you do not focus on me or the circumstances that are negative. They are only shared to show how mighty He is when He steps in. My prayer is that you see Him and what He did when He showed up. I pray you encounter Him in a way you haven't before and your relationship with Him will be stronger because of what you experience reading this book.

Enjoy the book!

The Best Is Yet to Come

7

Chapter 1

OPERATION CHRISTMAS CHILD

There comes a time in everyone's life when they encounter something that changes them forever, and for me, that was the ministry of Operation Christmas Child.

I had never heard of the ministry before. On a Sunday in 2001, sitting in a church pew, I heard presented for the first time the ministry of Operation Christmas Child. There was a couple from my church, Tom and Sheila, who had recently visited a church in nearby Traverse City and, while there, had been introduced to Operation Christmas Child.

The woman they heard speak in Traverse City was Sally Smith. Sally shared her experience with Operation Christmas Child and then presented a challenge to the congregation. Sally had heard Franklin Graham (founder of the ministry) speaking on a radio broadcast about collecting these "shoeboxes." The boxes (ideally the size and shape of a shoebox, though any similar box would suffice) are filled with items for a child, either boy or girl, ages 2–14. These boxes are then sent to over one hundred countries throughout the world and distributed to children who are in need due to poverty, war, famine, etc. Most have never received a gift before in their life. The best, and most important part, is that at the same time they receive the gift, they are also presented with the gospel message that Jesus loves them.

Sally decided that was something she would like to do. Because her financial situation was grim, she looked to and asked the Lord to fill ten shoeboxes. He didn't just fill her request. He also led her up and down the hollers of the Appalachian Mountains where she lived to ask her friends to fill shoeboxes as well. She filled a box truck and drove them to the collection center in Boone, North Carolina, to drop them off.

It was there that she met Franklin Graham. He was so impressed by her heart for the children that he invited her to travel to Bosnia with him to hand the boxes out. Later, he invited Sally to be a spokesperson for the ministry.

When Sally presented the ministry that day in Traverse City, she challenged those listening to fill ten shoeboxes themselves and to challenge everyone that they shared this with to fill ten. This was the ministry being presented at my church that day by Tom and Sheila. They were committing to fill ten boxes, and they echoed Sally's challenge to all who heard them speak to also fill ten boxes.

If this is the first time you have heard about Operation Christmas Child, I would like to encourage you to go to www.samaritanspurse.org. You just might discover something that will change your life as well. What I love most about it is that anyone can do it.

As we left the church and got into the van to head home, my four boys all talked about the Operation Christmas Child ministry. They said to me, "Mom, we would really like to do that. Can we please fill ten shoeboxes?"

I said, "Well, it's not that easy. It's going to cost a lot of money that I don't have. Let me pray about it, and I'll let you know."

The next day I said to the boys, "Okay, if you want to do this, I'm willing to do it, but we're going to have to pray and ask God to do it." I explained that we did not have the money it would take to buy the items needed to fill the boxes. We began to pray.

Within a day or two after we began to pray, I was at home and received a phone call from my neighbor Tammy. She owned a bakery in Detroit and would come up on the weekends and stay in a mobile home she owned next to our home.

When I answered the phone, she said, "Hello, Dianna. This is your neighbor, and I have a van load of toys. I'm on my way up north, and I don't know what to do with them. I prayed, and the Lord told me to call you, that you would know what to do with them."

I could not believe what I was hearing. God had heard and answered our prayers. I have to say in that moment, faith, prayer, and God himself became very real! I quickly told my neighbor all about Operation Christmas Child and how my sons and I had been praying. We had been asking God to fill ten shoeboxes, and we needed toys! I said to her, "Yes! We will take them. Please bring them over as soon as you get here."

A few hours later, she pulled up with her van. When I opened the back, what I saw just amazed me. The van was filled with antique toys, still in their original packaging. Immediately, I thought, *I could sell these antiques and make enough money to fill more than ten shoeboxes.*

I heard the Lord say, "No, you are to put these toys in the shoeboxes. You are not to sell them." I didn't understand at the time but came to understand later why He said that. I was able to fill our goal of ten shoeboxes, plus two additional boxes, plus we were able to give enough toys to Tom and Sheila for them to fill their twelve boxes.

I had a desire to fill the shoeboxes with more than toys. I wanted the children to also receive school supplies, candy, and hygiene items. Several of the toys from my neighbor were too big to put in the shoeboxes. I was able to sell them to an antique dealer for $250! That money was used for the school supplies, candy, hygiene items, and covered the shipping costs for our boxes as well as for Tom and Sheila's boxes.

When it was all over, for the first time in my life, I felt I had encountered the spirit of the Living God. I knew that He was real. I knew that He had heard my prayer and that He had answered it. I felt like I understood and experienced faith for the first time in my life. Up until this point in my life, I really did not have these things or even understand them. Needless to say, this experience radically changed my life and my walk with the Lord.

I took the shoeboxes to the relay center in town and dropped them off. When I came back home and walked through the door, I was all alone, and I remember distinctly hearing the voice of the Lord say to me, "This is your ministry." I was so happy and excited that He would call and allow me to serve Him in this way.

I said, "Yes, Lord, yes!" Looking back now, I am grateful that He did not show me at that moment what the next twelve years in the ministry would look like. I think if He had, I would have turned away from that call and not looked back.

At that time in my life, I was living in fear, self-doubt, and insecurity. Something about that whole experience led me to realize that I couldn't let my weaknesses hold me back. God had started to heal and deliver me from my fear and anxiety.

I knew that it was critical for me to just obey Him, and more healing would come. And it did! I went places and did things I never dreamed I would ever do in this ministry. All of it brought such freedom, joy, boldness, courage, strength, and a great peace. I was fully walking in His will, and there is no better place to be!

The following year, I said to the Lord, "If You would fill twelve boxes, why wouldn't You fill twenty-five? They are your children waiting to hear about you and how much you love them. You love them just as much as you love me."

So throughout the year, I would collect items for the shoeboxes. Wherever I was, I was always thinking of shoeboxes and purchasing items on sale for them.

I began petitioning people to give me their Beanie Babies collections. Many people had collected these popular small children's toys with the hopes of one day selling them and making a profit. Eventually, the craze subsided, and people were sitting on hundreds of Beanie Babies. When the word got out I was collecting them, they began to pour into my house. I felt like a faucet of Beanies got turned on above my house, and there was no end. It was amazing!

God answered my prayer once again and filled twenty-five shoeboxes. He brought me all the items that I needed and the shipping money to send them out that year. This was also the time I learned why He said that day to not sell the toys and put them in the boxes. He showed me that He sees and hears the child's prayer for items needed and wanted even though they have no clue a shoebox is coming to answer that prayer. At the same time, He sees you filling the box and lays on your heart what to put in it to meet that specific need or want. Only God can do this. We hear testimony after testimony from the children they received exactly what they had prayed for. So the toys I received that day were to fill a prayer request of a child! How cool is that?

I said, "Okay, God, let's fill fifty this next year!" He did. That was also the year my family moved from Bellaire to Traverse City.

A year prior, my husband had taken a job in Traverse City. We both made the decision we did not want to move to Traverse City. So for now, he would commute back and forth to work.

The Lord had other plans. He wanted us to make this move. We loved Bellaire and did not want to move, so we did not obey the Lord's prompting. He had a plan and a reason for us to move. I could not see what He was orchestrating or why.

Something started happening with some of our dearest friends that was not good and did not make sense. There were hard feelings and disagreements going on. One day, when I felt the situation was growing hopeless, I said, "Lord what is going on. Why is this happening?"

I felt Him answer right away, "I want you to move, and you are not listening or obeying me. So this is what I had to do to get your attention."

Wow, I was so ashamed at that moment. I realized that I had put my will above His. I got on my knees and repented before the Lord. I learned something that day about obedience. I want to obey the Lord when He is speaking. I don't want to suffer or see others suffer because of my lack of obedience. I want to obey Him and do His will.

We went to Traverse City to begin our search for a home. The first place that we looked at, we loved and wanted to put an offer in. Before we left the house, we circled up with the realtor and prayed, asking God to show us if this is where we were to live.

My second son said to me when we were done praying, "Mom, I have seen that scene before."

I said, "What?"

He said, "I have seen that scene before."

I responded, "I have no idea what you are talking about. What do you mean?"

He said, "About a year ago, I had a dream, and we were standing in that house, in that circle, praying with that realtor."

I was blown away by what he said. I realized the God of the universe was communicating directly to my family that this is where He wanted us to live!

When we put an offer in, the realtor said to us, "I was so sick of having so many offers come in on that home and even going up to the closing table and walking away with no deal. I was just about to drop the listing because of this, but I'm so glad I didn't."

When I heard that, I felt the Lord show me that He literally held that home for us and would not allow anyone else to purchase it. It was for us. I truly believe God plucks and plants people in and out of homes. He places us where He wants us. What an incredible feeling to know that. Within three weeks of our accepted offer, we closed on the house and were moving in just before the school year started in 2002.

One year after we moved, I became the collection center coordinator for the Traverse City area, and our home became the collection center site for Operation Christmas Child. It was then I realized this was why God wanted us to move to Traverse City.

As a collection center, we would receive boxes from all of Northern Michigan. They would come to our home, and we would put them in a shipping carton. Once in the carton, they were loaded into a semitrailer sitting in our front yard. They would then be transported to the nearest processing center.

I did not have experience with semitrailers to know that when you drop the front legs down, you need to put support underneath them. If you don't, they are going to sink into the ground from the weight being loaded if they are not on cement or asphalt. The trailers were on our front lawn, so that's exactly what happened.

I watched in horror as the two trailers filled with shoeboxes almost tipped over in my yard. This happened on the scheduled day for pick up. We were up till one in the morning trying to get these trailers unstuck.

When we finally got the trailers unstuck, I went in the house and crawled into bed. I began to laugh. I could see the enemy's hand at work. He wanted to stop these shoeboxes from getting into the hands of the children and perhaps to discourage me enough that I would quit. I determined right then and there I would not allow this to hinder or stop me from continuing on in what God had called me to.

It's so important to know God has called you to do something before you enter into it. The reason is when things go wrong, and they will, you can stand in faith knowing God is with you.

The following year, I said, "God, if You would fill fifty, why not a hundred?" He did! The next year, "if You would fill a hundred, why not two hundred?" He filled five hundred instead!

That year, I had the privilege of volunteering at the processing plant in Minnesota. This is the next step on the journey for the shoeboxes. This is where they take out the shipping money from each box and make sure that there's no chocolates or liquid items that are not allowed. They are then taped shut, ready for their destination. These shoeboxes go to over a hundred different countries.

It's not just a feel-good Christmas gift box, but along with it, they receive a booklet printed in their own language of the birth, life, death, and resurrection of Jesus. The children are given the opportunity to accept Jesus as their Savior.

So many do come to know Him right then. I think it is because they can feel His love at that moment as He is revealing Himself to them. It opens their heart to receive Him. It is just such an incredible ministry.

In 2016, Operation Christmas Child collected 11.4 million shoeboxes for the children. I know of no other ministry that can reach that many children in one year.

While I was at the Minnesota processing plant, I saw something that really got my attention. There were huge boxes filled with hand-knit sweaters waiting to be placed in the shoeboxes. They were such beautiful sweaters and so well-made by women all over the United States.

I felt the Lord give me an idea. "Go back home and go on the local Christian radio station and petition women to begin knitting, crocheting, and sewing items for the shoeboxes." I did just that.

I had no idea the response that I would get. My phone for the next two weeks began ringing off the hook. Women and even men began to knit and crochet washcloths, little sweaters, mittens, hats, and even purses. They were sewing bags, purses, small security blankets and making wooden toys and jump ropes. It was absolutely amazing the items that came in, thousands of them throughout the year.

We were also accepting donations throughout the year of used items. We would sell the items at garage sales to raise the funds to purchase items and to help cover the shipping costs for the boxes.

The next year, we were at one thousand shoeboxes.

I found out in December of that year that I was chosen to go to Jamaica to hand the shoeboxes out to the children. The ministry felt it was important for me as the leader to experience every part of the journey of a shoebox. I could lead my team members better with that experience under my belt.

What an incredible trip it was. We went in February, and our first day of distribution was February 14, Valentine's Day.

The children at school were learning all about love for Valentine's Day. We showed up out of nowhere with a van load of shoeboxes filled with love.

The first place that we stopped, the children were all squealing with excitement! The teachers were trying to get them to settle and quiet down. The teacher said, "Children, children, God's word says we must treat strangers very, very good because they could be angels unaware."

When she said that, the children's eyes bugged out of their heads and their mouths fell open and they looked at us and they really thought we were angels. Most of these children had never seen a white person before in their lives. As we were standing there before them, they literally thought we were angels.

As I saw what was happening to the children, I had goosebumps going up and down my arms and legs. I felt like I was an angel! It was truly an amazing moment that I will never forget.

After handing out all the boxes, a young boy came running up to me and said, "Miss, Miss!"

I said, "What's the matter?" I could tell he was upset about something.

He said, "I didn't get a letter. I didn't get a letter." And he started to cry.

When you make these shoeboxes up, they encourage you to write a letter to the children and send a picture of yourself. What I found is most of these children do not have parents or grandparents. They really don't have anyone to love them. So when you send a shoebox, you become their mother, father, brother, sister, uncle, grandma, grandpa, or new best friend. Often, the letter and picture mean more to them than the shoebox or the items inside, even though these children have nothing.

I made a vow to the Lord that day. When I returned home, I would give the message, "Write a letter or note and put a picture of yourself in the box. It means everything to the child."

The children were so grateful for every single thing in their boxes. We found several children, when opening their box, took one item out and tried to pass the box onto the next child. They had no idea they got to keep the whole box for themselves. They are so used to sharing and not having much. They were in shock when told "This is all for you!"

After a week of distributing over ten thousand boxes, it was time to go back home. It was a cherished trip and an amazing chapter in my life!

The next year, we filled two thousand shoeboxes, and the year after that, over five thousand! That year, I had the privilege of volunteering at the Atlanta processing center. Try to imagine walking into a room containing over a million shoeboxes, each one a different shape, with individually selected items, and all wrapped in different Christmas paper.

I walked up to a pallet that had probably about ten layers of shoeboxes on it. As I stood there staring at all the shoeboxes, the Lord spoke to me. He said, "Those shoeboxes represent the children. They are beautiful, and they come in all shapes, sizes, and colors. Each one is very unique." I thought it was a beautiful picture that He was speaking about His children.

I really enjoy volunteering at the processing centers because you get to see all the things people put in their shoeboxes. You can get some great ideas for filling your own shoeboxes. It's also an opportunity to experience being around hundreds of people with the same passion. If you ever have the opportunity to go, I encourage you to go.

At the end of the year, I felt the Lord speak to me to start a nonprofit. The name of it was to be Unlimited Hidden Treasures. It would be a resale store to fund filling shoeboxes throughout the year. I filled out all the paperwork and then waited for God to open the door for that to happen. In the waiting, we continued to operate by having garage sales to fund the boxes and collect new items to put in the shoeboxes.

In 2009, our last year that we did packing parties, we filled ten thousand shoeboxes. For everything, there is a season. I felt the Lord say the season for packing parties is over, and now you are to focus on building up the team of volunteers that I had been working with and overseeing.

In 2011, I became a regional area coordinator, and I was traveling four weeks out of the year. Like I said in the beginning, I had no idea the day that the Lord called me into the ministry what all that would entail. It has been worth every minute that I have spent with this ministry. It has changed my life!

Throughout that nine years of packing parties and filling all those shoeboxes, there was never a time that we were lacking anything. God provided all we needed.

I liked to put thirteen items in each shoebox, and then there was the shipping money. God would bring all of that in one form or another. Miracles were a part of my everyday life. What an adventure waking up and saying to God, "What will you bring to me today?"

In the beginning of 2013, I went through a divorce. I felt the Lord ask me to step down and away from the ministry as I walked through that process. He did reassure me that there would be a time that I would come back. When I did, I would pick up where I left off.

For now, I want to take you back to the beginning of my life where it all began.

Chapter 2

YOUNGER YEARS

Looking back, I feel that my life was very simple. I grew up in Central Lake, Michigan, a typical small town where everyone knew everyone. The town consisted of a gas station, a small grocery store, and a library. There wasn't really a lot for kids to do.

I was part of a very large family. There were eight siblings—three boys and five girls. I was number seven in the line. We lived on a small farm and had a very large garden. That garden, along with a few fruit trees, would produce over a thousand quarts of food a year. That would keep us fed each winter, until the next planting season. Our food was as organic as it gets, and I believe that's why all of us are still very healthy today.

When you're in a family that size, there is always work to do, and everyone has their part to play. We lived on three and a half wooded acres with a creek running through the back. Imagination, adventure, and exploration was what kept us occupied.

I can remember playing by the creek, making mud pies for hours. I remember every time we would go outside to play, my mother would say, "Stay away from that creek!" I'm ashamed to admit it, but that was the first place we would go. We just had to make sure she couldn't see us from the house.

If you know the story of Joseph in the Bible, I would say that my life mirrored his. Like him, I was a dreamer, tattler and was accused of being a mommy and daddy's girl.

From the time I was little, the Lord would speak to me through dreams. I'm not sure why I felt it necessary to tattle on my brothers and sisters, getting them into trouble. For some reason, my brothers and sisters always felt that I was favored by my mom and dad. I would get called Mommy's girl, a "Goody Two-shoes," and "you think you're special."

I didn't have anything in me to want to be naughty or break rules. I always wanted to be good, and I felt that if I was good, I would be loved and accepted.

Because I tattled on my brothers and sisters, they didn't like me very much. In fact, I think they hated me at times. I think they really did not want me around, and I can understand why. I was alone a lot, and during those years of loneliness, feelings of rejection and inferiority settled over me.

I felt the same way at school. I was not popular, and I didn't have a lot of friends. Life was hard because I always felt like I didn't belong. I was an outsider, looked at as weird or different. I think these feelings of unworthiness became the foundation for my depression.

There was something else different about me. I could see, hear, and feel in the spirit realm. Now at the time, when I was young, I didn't know that's what it was. I didn't understand it, so it was very scary at times. It wasn't until I was older that I began to understand I have spiritual giftings. I am very sensitive to the spirit realm and, I believe, prophetic. As a child, these things were hard, confusing, and scary. I had no one to turn to, to ask questions or to teach me in this.

I had two encounters when I was younger that were so traumatic that they set in motion a depression and fear that shadowed me for years.

The first experience happened when I was sleeping between my two sisters on the bed we shared. I was about nine years old. In the middle of the night, I went into a dream that turned into a physical manifestation.

I saw a very large hairy, clawed hand coming down out of the sky, and it came down onto my right arm. It dug its claws into my flesh starting at my wrist and went up my arm. The pain woke me up. I looked down at my arm and blood had been drawn in three lines. This was not just a dream; this was a real demonic encounter physically.

I was so scared I could hardly breathe. I didn't know what to do. I couldn't move, and I remember just getting down underneath the covers to hide. I do not remember being able to sleep the rest of the night. When morning came, there was a fear in me that was paralyzing. I was too scared to share this with anyone because I knew that they would think I was crazy. I was so scared of being "locked up." The other incident followed shortly.

I lay in my bed, trying to fall asleep, but sleep did not come. Out of nowhere, I had a vision. I saw the world spinning like a globe, and I heard three questions asked: Who are you? Where did you come from? Where are you going?

The moment the first question was asked, I felt a physical tingling feeling starting at my toes, and it went all the way up and consumed my entire body. I had no control over that feeling at all. It was just there. Along with it was a fear that enveloped my entire body. I was frozen in fear. I could hardly breathe. I didn't understand. I didn't know where it came from. I couldn't answer the questions. I was so young. I felt completely helpless.

Those two things that happened to me on separate occasions left me with a fear that would come on my body and, at times, physically paralyze me. I could not eat or sleep or function in a normal manner. I was afraid of everybody and everything. It was so horrible and very real. I just didn't understand and felt I had no one I could turn to who would understand or could help me. I felt this was something I would have to learn to live with the rest of my life.

My mother took me to the doctor, and they did a lot of testing. They basically said to my mom they wanted to keep me because I was on the verge of a breakdown. I knew if my mother allowed them to keep me, I would never go home again. My mother said, "No, I'm going to take her home, and we'll work through this." I was so thankful when she said no.

At the time, whenever I would think about these experiences, I would feel such shame and embarrassment. I was living in constant fear that prevented me from being able to talk to anyone about what

I had experienced. I did not realize until later that this was the work of the enemy. It is his method to keep you stuck. You don't get help because of shame. So you can't get out of it. He comes to kill, steal, and destroy, and that was what he was trying to do to me. I didn't and couldn't see at that time that this was the beginning of a fight to hold onto my very life.

The enemy sought to take my life at every opportunity he could. He wanted me dead, depressed, full of fear, full of anger, and just plain lost. It's so hard to believe he would target me so young. I did not ask for, nor was I delving into anything that would cause these things to happen. I was innocent.

When I look at my life now and the ministry that I was called to, it makes sense why I was targeted. Millions of children hear the gospel message every year through Operation Christmas Child. It would be years before I would get involved with this ministry, but God was using all of this to train me for the ministry in the future. You will learn more about this in chapter 17.

I was raised in a Christian home. We went to church Sunday morning and night. I had a friend, and his mother would pick me up every Wednesday night for Awana Clubs. I was being taught and raised in a Christian environment.

I was taking it in but not applying it or living it. When these demonic things happened to me, I began to move toward God for help. That move was out of fear at the time, but I'm glad that it pushed me toward Him. Otherwise, I would have continued on the way that I was.

I felt most of my childhood and teen years we're clouded in fear, shame, loneliness, emptiness, depression, pain, and suicidal thoughts. I did not want to die, but I wanted all those things to stop. I accepted the Lord as my Savior when I was a senior, and I felt only a small change in my life. I guess you could say that I just ran to God out of fear, but I really did not understand or know Him. That would come later.

I am eternally grateful for the Awana program that I attended on Wednesday nights. I spent hours memorizing scripture verses and reading the Bible to get points, suckers, and charms. If I had not gone to Awana Clubs, I would not have the word inside of me like I do today. So I am a firm believer even if kids are memorizing scripture for points, suckers, and charms, so be it. It is easier to memorize when you are young, and His words will not return void.

I did not know or realize at the time I was going through the hard stuff that God was always there. He was always with me, and He never left me. At the time, it did not seem like that at all. I was always crying out for Him, and I really didn't feel or see Him, so I thought He wasn't there. But I realize now that He was.

I would have to say that as a child and teen, I was living in what I would call religion and tradition, following rules and trying to be good. I always wanted to please. I realize now that that is all worthless, and it's not about being good and obeying the rules; it's about a relationship. I did not find that out until later.

Leaving my childhood and entering into adulthood, I did not see much change in my internal issues. I was having small breakthroughs here and there that helped me to keep going. They would give me hope that soon, I could just be normal like everyone else.

I am now beginning to think about getting married and having a family. My heart's desire was to be a stay-at-home mom, raise my children, and possibly homeschool.

I only dated one guy in high school. I'm not even sure I would call it dating. He was a good friend, and we did a lot together. That did not last long at all. In fact, it ended the day of my graduation from high school.

I graduated and went right to work at Second Chance. It was a company that made bulletproof vests. That is where I learned to sew using a commercial machine. Those machines are a hundred times faster than a normal machine. It took me a month and lots of tears to get it down. I was at that job right up until I got married.

So it's only fitting to start the next chapter where a new chapter began in my life.

Chapter 3

MARRIED LIFE

I met my husband one year after graduating from high school. We dated for about two months when he proposed. We were married eight months later.

I was twenty years old when I got married. I was very young, naïve, and immature. I was also still dealing with all those issues. That was no one's fault but mine. I experienced a lot of rejection and inferiority in my growing up years. So when my future husband came along and accepted me and loved me, I was hooked. Not only was I accepted, I was made to feel like a princess. It was almost scary because I had never been treated that way before. I loved it, but there were many signs of things not being right that I either ignored or just didn't want to see. I think I was caught up in feeling so loved and accepted that I just looked over any red flags.

The first five years of marriage were like a whirlwind. We both agreed to wait five years to have kids. We would both work a lot to get ahead so I could stay home when we started having kids.

Our first home was in Cedar Springs, Michigan. We were given a twelve-by-forty-five single wide mobile home trailer for our wedding gift. It needed a lot of work, but I was never afraid of work. We were there for only a few months and decided to move back to Bellaire where most of our family lived.

We were there for only a few months and then bought a very run-down motel in Charlevoix. We used our trailer as a down payment. That adventure lasted about one and a half years.

We sold the motel and settled into a rented trailer for a short time before our next move. We then purchased a milk distribution business. Each time we bought and sold, we made a nice profit to roll over into the next purchase. It was slowly bringing us to our goal of getting ahead. Soon I could stay home and start having babies.

Our five-year agreement of waiting to have children had arrived. I was now pregnant with our first child. He was born just a few months before we sold the business.

Within a very short time after selling the business, something happened that began to change the course of my life. The person we sold the business to decided not to pay us the monthly payment. We had no secured agreement in our contract, so there was nothing we could do. To make a long story short, we lost the business and had to walk away from all equity that we had acquired over the last five years. Our home was the only thing we were able to keep. Everything else, we lost.

My world was turned upside down. Everything I had put my *trust* and *security* in was now all gone. Five years of working two and three jobs at a time, buying dumps, fixing them up, and selling them for a profit gone—all gone overnight. What happened to us was unreal. We didn't ask for it. We didn't create it, and there was nothing we could do about it.

With my two-month-old baby lying on my lap, I looked up at God and said, "Why?" This was the worst thing that ever happened to me up to this point in my life.

I felt Him answer immediately, "You had placed your *trust* and *security* for the future in money and getting ahead with no thought of Me. You had it all figured out. I have been blessing you all along the way, but your eyes began to focus on the next sale, the next profit. You lost sight of Me being your provider and My plans for your life."

I didn't realize I had done this. I could see in that moment how He was there for me. He loved me, and He had to get my attention to stop me from going any further down that path.

I am so thankful that God intervened in my life! I was headed down a horrible path, not even seeing it, and it would have gone on if He hadn't intervened. So what I thought was the worst thing to ever happen yet was really the best thing that had happened! It made me realize I was still walking in religion and tradition only. I didn't really know Him.

I didn't want to live that way anymore. I wanted to look to Him and ask Him what to do. It should not be me figuring it out. From here on out, I was going to seek Him and get to know Him whatever it took.

No longer would I look to man, government, or the world to be my provider. I would look to God. I wanted to really get to know Him and have deep intimacy with Him. I wanted the abundant life that Scripture talks about and rivers of living water flowing from my innermost being.

Something that could and should have devastated me and sent me down a path of depression did the opposite. It drove me to know Him deeper. It also created a hunger and thirst for Him that is still going today. I realized that is exactly what He wanted to happen out of this crisis. I chose not to go down but up.

Every human being is faced with choices every day. We get to choose. We are not robots. Here's what I've learned about this. Whether the choice is teeny tiny or an enormous one, we get to choose how we will handle situations. We can choose fear, anger, bitterness, or unforgiveness which leads directly to death. Or we can choose faith, joy, hope, and forgiveness which leads to life. I'm not saying it's easy to choose the right response, but it is our choice. We cannot blame anyone else for our choice. A very dear friend of mine said to me, "It's your attitude and your actions that will determine your outcome." I have found that to be so true.

The babies began to come one after another. I had four sons, and between the last two, I lost a baby two months along.

It was a sea of changing diapers, laundry, and getting up in the night for feedings.

There was so little personal time for me, but I tried every chance I got to get into the word, prayer, and just spending time with Him. My love began to grow for Him. I was seeking Him more and more. When my youngest son was born, I encountered the Spirit of the Living God like never before.

Chapter 4

ENCOUNTER WITH GOD

The church that I was attending at this time was mostly young people but had a group of elderly people as well. It was at this time that I began really hungering and thirsting for more of God. I actually said to the Lord, "If this was all that there was to You, then just take me home." I felt so dry about the Lord spiritually. But at the same time, I was hungering and thirsting for more. I didn't know at the time He was placing that hunger in me. He was drawing me in.

Not long after I began having these feelings, someone in the church who I had known for a long time approached me and said, "How are you doing?" I somehow knew the question was not physically how are you doing but spiritually. I began to pour out my heart that I was very dissatisfied with where I was at and that there just had to be more!

The person who spoke to me acted a little shocked and said, "Wow, I can't believe what you're saying! I have spoken to several of our friends, and they were literally saying the same thing you had just said. I am thinking of starting a group at the church that would meet on Saturday nights to worship and pray. Would you be interested in going?"

I was very excited, and I said, "Yes!"

I felt that this was God moving because of everyone feeling the same way. He was calling us to Him! He was placing that hunger in us because we cannot even hunger for Him on our own.

November 1999, just after Thanksgiving, we began to meet at our church on Saturday nights, late, around 9:30 p.m. The person who was heading it owned a pizza shop. We had to wait until he closed to then meet together. We would worship for about an hour with taped music that was coming out of the Brownsville revival in Florida. When we were done worshipping, we would circle up and pray for each other, for our community, and for our world leaders.

We did this for about seven weeks. On the eighth week, January 15, 2000, the Spirit of the Living God showed up like I had never experienced before in my life. It was so amazing, and it changed me forever. I was struggling so bad with my internal issues and my marriage, but God was getting ready to change that.

The group brought me to the front of the church on the stage, and I was being prayed over by them all. I lifted my hands to the Lord in full surrender to Him. The next thing I knew, I was on the floor, and when I came up, I began to speak in a heavenly language. I knew at that moment that I did not have to live in fear, depression, anxiety, and anger anymore. I knew there was an answer and a way out. I had hope for the first time ever in my life. I didn't know what it was then, but I knew it would be revealed down the road.

That night, there were about twenty-five young people my age, and they all received prayer. They went down under the power of the Holy Spirit and began to speak in another language.

None of us in that room were Pentecostal and did not have a background or teaching of it. We knew that what was happening to us was very real and of the Lord. I didn't want to leave because the presence of God was so thick I just wanted to linger in it. We did not leave the church until three o'clock in the morning! I just knew that my life from that moment on was going to be different.

I was experiencing things like hearing His voice, having visions, and physical manifestation of His presence. These were all things I experienced before but did not understand. I now understood everything. It all made sense. I knew what it was. That is what happens when you receive the baptism of the Holy Spirit. He is your teacher, guide, and truth giver.

I was awakened at eight ten the next morning. There are times when I look at the clock, and I know God is referring to a scripture. This time it was Hebrews 8:10 (NASB),

> For this is the covenant that I will make with the house of Israel after those days, says the Lord: I will put My laws in their mind and write them on their hearts; and I will be their God, and they shall be My people. None of them shall teach his neighbor, and none his brother, saying, "Know the Lord," for all shall know Me, from the least of them to the greatest of them.

I also knew and was aware that there were a lot of things in my life that needed to change. If I surrendered, God would begin that work in my life. It makes me think of the scripture Philippians 1:6 (NASB), "He who began a good work in me will be faithful to complete it until the day of Jesus Christ."

The next morning, after being filled with the Holy Spirit, I was back in church by 9:00 a.m. I was so excited for my newfound friend and experience with the Holy Spirit. I couldn't wait to share with my friends that weren't with us what had happened.

When the older people in the congregation heard about what had happened that night, they were very upset. They said that it was of the devil, and we were not allowed to practice or teach anything that had happened to us that night. The church doctrine spoke against it. I was in shock. The very thing that had just set me free and would change my life forever I was not allowed to share or talk about. It was unreal.

There was one more thing that I experienced the morning after the encounter. It was a vision.

I saw myself standing at the edge of the ocean, and I had a teaspoon in my hand. I reached down, and I dipped the spoon into the water and brought it back up. As I was looking at the spoonful of water, the Lord spoke to me and said, "This is all that you got of Me last night. This is what is available to you if you want it." When He spoke the last line, I was looking out at the vast ocean before me. It took my breath away from what He just said to me. The experience I had that night was so amazing and profound; how could I ever handle more? An ocean full of Him? Wow!

I realized that I couldn't handle more of Him in the state that I was in. He began working deep in my soul and spirit man to change and clean me. It's then that I would be able to handle more of God. That is exactly what I wanted and had longed for. I was so excited to finally come to a place where I could begin having more of God.

Besides the ocean vision, He also spoke to me about that cleanup process. I had just poured myself a cup of tea that was extremely hot. As you all know, you can't gulp it down. You have to take very small sips. As I was getting ready to take a sip, I said to the Lord, "Please clean me up quickly! Just get it all over with! Remove all the sin and strongholds in my life as fast as You can. I'm ready and want to be changed from within."

He spoke to me clearly and said, "Just as you have to sip the tea so that you don't burn your mouth, so too I will have to slowly remove the things from your life. You could not handle it or survive it being taken away all at once."

I was very discouraged and frustrated when He said that. I didn't understand it either, but as He began that work in me, I quickly understood as it was so incredibly painful.

As He removes the things that are not of Him, you are actually dying to self. I had to die to my selfish wants and desires, and the pain is like you are physically dying—which you are! It was then that I could begin to see and understand what He had said to me that morning. He would have to do it slowly. It's the only way I could handle it!

Removing mindsets that had been there since childhood does not happen overnight. It just took time, a very long process but so worth every minute of it. The work would take years!

One of my first learning experiences about the Holy Spirit was about lying. Shortly after being Spirit-filled, I was experiencing with one of my sons a time of him lying to me. I could never catch him in it or prove it. It was very frustrating.

31

I learned that the Holy Spirit is truth, and He is the giver of truth through a story in Stormie Omartian's book *Power of a Praying Mom*. She was experiencing the same thing. Her son was lying to her also. She said the Lord showed her through the Word that the Holy Spirit is truth and gives truth. So when her son lied to her again, she asked the Holy Spirit to show her the truth, and He did. I was so excited about this.

The next time my son lied to me, and I knew it but couldn't prove it, I put into practice what I had learned. I prayed to the Holy Spirit to please reveal to me the truth of this situation. That is exactly what happened. The Holy Spirit revealed the truth.

I went to my son and I confronted him about the lying and I told him I knew the truth. I explained to him how I had just learned that the Holy Spirit is truth, and He is the giver of truth. "I put it into practice and prayed and asked Him to reveal the truth to me if you were lying, and He did."

I then shared the truth with my son, and he could not deny it! You should have seen the look on his face when I shared all of this with him. I told my son, "You now have fair warning that you cannot lie to me again because the Holy Spirit is going to show me the truth."

He continued to lie, and the Spirit continued to show me the truth. Each time, I would call him out on it. After a while, my son finally realized he had to just give it up. He realized he wasn't going to win. He stopped lying to me.

During this time of encountering the Lord, hearing His voice, feeling His presence, having dreams and visions, I found it very important to begin journaling it all. I'm so thankful that I did because you can forget so easily, and this is literally how I wrote this book. I could go back to my journal entries to write out the story that you are now reading.

I want to encourage you to journal your experiences with God. You can go back in times of discouragement and be encouraged by His faithfulness.

As I began drawing closer and closer to the Lord, I felt that my husband was too at first. Then something scared him that triggered him to turn away and not come back.

He was experiencing deep visions that he would go out under the power of the Holy Spirit, visions that were very detailed and prophetic showing future things. At first he received them, but then they scared him. He shut them off. He said no when the next one started to come. In a sense, he shut off the Holy Spirit to his life. From that point on, things progressively got worse in our marriage. It could be the only outcome when you have two people going in opposite directions.

Chapter 5

BIG CHANGE COMING

Within a month, I found out my husband had a completely separate life that I knew nothing about. He had a separate PO box and credit cards in his name only. So he was carrying on another life apart from me.

The Holy Spirit revealed to the pastor of the church we were attending that he was living this separate life. The pastor came to the house and confronted him. My husband denied the claims, and so the pastor left. When he was driving down the road to go home, the Holy Spirit said, "You are not done. Go back and ask him if he knows who Ananias and Sapphira were." If you don't know the story in the Bible, you need to take a minute to go read it. It is found in Acts 5:1–11. It basically is a husband and wife lying to the church. They both dropped dead on the spot by God.

When the pastor came back and asked him a second time, he lied again. Pastor then asked him if he knew who Ananias and Sapphira were.

He said, "No." He was not reading his Bible, so he would not know who they were or the story about them.

Pastor said, "Well, I'm not telling you that you're going to drop dead right now, but you better stop lying. You need to confess to your wife what you have done." He told him that he would be checking to see if he had told me.

My husband came to me and confessed what he had done, but there was no godly repentance, only worldly sorrow. This is found in

2 Corinthians 7:10 (NASB), "For the sorrow that is according to the will of God produces a repentance without regret, leading to salvation; but the sorrow of the world produces death." I look back now and realize this was the time that I should have left him and divorced.

What happened next was, instead of hiding the second life, he did it all in front of me. There was strong pride and arrogance in him. I was told by him, "I will live my life the way I want to and make my own choices without you. It's just the way it is. You have to conform to my way. If you don't like it, you can leave."

This led to a division between us. At one point, I actually said to him, "There is a chasm between us that is getting wider and wider with no bridge."

He felt free and very happy to go on living the way he wanted to without having to worry about hiding anything. Whenever I would confront him on issues, I basically was told to be quiet, mind my own business, and leave him alone. It was extremely hard.

There was also an addiction of spending. He would spend more than we had the money to pay for. I was doing the checkbook at the time, and it came to the point where I had to just turn it over to him and let him do whatever he was going to do. I was not going to accept the responsibility of trying to pay bills that he created that we didn't have the money to pay.

This really set him off because there wouldn't be anyone to blame then when the money wasn't there to pay the bills. It took me out of the picture.

From then on, it just got progressively worse every day. There really was nothing left to our marriage. We were two people living under the same roof.

One day, I was listening to our local Christian radio station. They were hosting an author, Jan Silvious. She was being interviewed about her new book *Foolproofing Your Life*.

When the interview started and the questions were asked and she would answer them, I stood in shock at what I was hearing. It was my life. It was what I was living in and with. I felt the book was an answer and hope for me. I sent for the book.

When it came, and I read through it, I was amazed. It answered so many questions. It taught me how to stay in a marriage living with a person who chooses foolish behavior every day. This book really saved my life. It taught me how to handle and respond to someone who willingly makes foolish choices every day. It gave me clarity, hope, peace, and sanity.

I highly recommend this book to everyone, believer or nonbeliever. It gives you the tools to handle a person in your life who has foolish behavior. Foolish behavior is self-focused and includes lying, controlling, manipulating, and cheating.

I shared with you earlier that when we lost our business, God pointed out to me I was trusting in man and money for my provision. It was a turning point for me in my faith. My faith began to grow. I had to look to my Father for my provision. Well, when my husband chose to remain in his foolish behavior, my faith had to move to a whole new level.

I was not working at the time. I was a stay-at-home mom volunteering full-time in Operation Christmas Child.

My husband was accusing me of spending too much money so he couldn't pay the bills. The money issues were because of his addictions. So he said, "I am going to put you on an allowance." He figured out the mileage to go to church, store, and to take my kids to school. I would get enough gas money for that only and some grocery money. Nothing else. Many times that was not enough money to pay for everything.

So faith was my go-to. I had to go to my Heavenly Father to get my needs met. I did not tell other people my needs, only God.

When I didn't have enough grocery money, I would cry out to Him to bring me meat. That's the most expensive thing on the grocery list, so that is what I asked for. He would deliver it right to my door. My friend, whose husband would go out and hunt game, would bring that meat to me. I began looking to my Heavenly Father for provision because my earthly husband would not provide. My friend did not know I had prayed for meat.

My other friend put in a garden and would bring me fresh produce all the time. I did not ask her for it.

One time, my mom bought some new underwear but discovered they were the wrong size. She did not want to take them back and asked me if I wanted them. She didn't know I had prayed for them.

Other times, my friend at work would get fresh farm eggs and give them to me free. The person that she got them from, their chickens were just producing more than they could get rid of.

God was faithful in providing answers to my specific prayer requests. One particular request was answered in a hilarious way. I needed six dollars to buy pie crusts to make up one pie for us and one to give away to someone. I didn't have the money. I prayed once again that God would provide.

My husband had spilled milk on the carpet in our living room and did not clean it up. The next day, it smelled so bad, and I was very upset and told him he needed to clean the carpet. He was very angry with me that I was asking him to clean it up. He did relent and rented a Rug Doctor and cleaned the carpet. After cleaning the carpet, however, he refused to return the rented cleaner. He demanded that I do it.

I said, "No, you take it back."

He refused. He walked out of the house and said, "It's your problem. You take it back!" I took it back.

I did not know there was a five-dollar deposit that you got back once you returned it. With that five dollars, I thought, *I have almost what I need to buy my pie crust.* I hoped maybe I would have enough change in my purse to get to the six dollars I needed.

I went to the store, grabbed the crust, and started for the cash register. When I turned around and started down an aisle, there was a dollar bill lying on the floor. I picked it up and looked all around to see if there was anyone there that I could give the dollar back to. There wasn't, and I literally laughed out loud and said, "Only You, God, only You!" He brought me the dollar that I needed to purchase the pie crust.

I could go on and on with miraculous stories of how God would provide for me. It really increased my faith and my intimacy with Him. It gave me hope and increased my desire for more of Him.

That has never stopped. My faith grows every day because of Him and what He does. He is so amazing!

Whatever my husband took away, I would no longer fight with him or beg him. I would just say "Okay" and then I would turn around and lay the matter before the Lord. I would tell Him my needs, and He never failed. He always came through for me.

Because I was volunteering full-time with the ministry Operation Christmas Child, I needed a phone and a vehicle to carry supplies for the ministry. I also needed a place to operate, store items, and room to pack the boxes. We had a thirty-by-forty pole barn on our property where I set the operation up.

One by one, my husband began to take each of these things away from me. He took the phone away first. My sister came to me and said, "I am paying for a phone for you for the year." It was a Skype phone so that I could continue in the ministry.

Next, my husband kicked me out of the pole barn that we owned and said I could not use it anymore; it was his, and he didn't want me in it anymore. God provided two semitrailers that were free storage from a local business that leases storage units.

He then took away all my gas money to use for the vehicle for the ministry. My friends began to give me the money that I needed to put in the vehicle so that I could continue working in the ministry. It was an amazing time to see God's hand move and provide, but at the same time, it was extremely hard because of the abuse that I was receiving from my husband. It was heaven and hell at the same time. I felt like a ping-pong ball being hit back and forth between the two worlds.

From the time I got married, I loved my husband. I wanted to be a good wife, and I believed in the sanctity of marriage and the vow that I had taken to stay with my husband until death did us part. I took that very seriously, but my eyes began to open to the truth that I was living in a very abusive situation. There was lying, controlling, manipulating, and unfaithfulness going on.

I realized I had idolized him and my marriage, and God began to open my eyes to see the truth. And it's the truth that will set you free. I began to implement what I learned in the book *Foolproofing*

Your Life. As I began to do that, I was receiving peace, discernment, clarity, understanding, and hope that I did not have before.

The author of the book comes right out and says the book is not about pushing divorce. It's about helping you to determine if this person has foolish behavior or is an actual fool. If they are, is God telling you to stay or go? If He is telling you to stay, then it gives you the tools to help you do that.

Well, like I said earlier, I felt I idolized my marriage and my husband, but I did not realize it at the time. I should have divorced when I found out he was living two lives, but because of that idolization and a huge fear, I didn't do it.

As I began growing in my relationship and intimacy with the Lord, my eyes began to be opened. The scales were coming off, and the veil was being lifted to see the truth. I began to see where I was at, where he was, and what was happening in our marriage. Because of that, the control and manipulation was not working for him anymore. I began to see it and not participate in it. He didn't know what to do with me. He began to distance himself even further from me.

I then had two dreams that were from the Lord showing me what He was doing and what my husband would choose to do next. It was the Lord sovereignly stepping in and protecting myself and my sons.

This is my first dream. I was asleep in bed in our bedroom with my husband. He was asleep as well. I woke up, and I went into our attached bathroom. The sewer was coming up in the sink, toilet, and tub. The tub was half full of sewer when I ran to wake my husband up. He was upset that I had awakened him. I told him there was a problem in the bathroom, and he needed to come and fix it.

He walked in and saw the sewer and said, "So? It will go away!" He walked out of the bathroom and went back to sleep. When he left, the sewer went down a couple of inches in the bathtub. When the sewer went down, I saw bloodsuckers on the side of the tub. The dream ended.

The interpretation of the dream:

-   The sewage is the demonic activity that my husband was involved in.

39

- It now is rising to the level of affecting the whole family.
- God is now going to step in and protect us.

This is the second dream. I was standing outside of a convenience store, and I had on a pair of purple overalls with a white shirt. Three men that looked exactly alike, dressed in business suits, we're having a conversation together right outside the store. When they were done talking, they started toward the store to talk to me. The men were now standing in front of me. They said to me, "We have talked among ourselves, and we have decided that you are going to be in charge now permanently. The owner has left, and we are putting you in charge." They left, and I went inside. As I went through the store door, I headed to the back room. As I entered the back room, I was entering into a school classroom with children present. I knew that I was the teacher. The dream ended.

The interpretation of the dream:

- The three men are the Father, Son, and Holy Spirit.
- Me in purple overalls and white shirt—purple is royalty, and white is righteousness. I was under the authority of Christ covered in His righteousness. Overalls means ready to work.
- The convenience store represents my home.
- The classroom with children represented the ministry, Operation Christmas Child, that I was involved in at the time.

Within three days of having the last dream, my husband came to me and said, "I'm leaving. I've taken a job in Detroit, and I want you and the boys to go with me."

I knew at that moment that I was not to follow him. I was reminded of the two dreams, and I knew this was God removing him from the home to protect the family. The dreams were playing out.

I said, "I cannot do that. I will not do that. I will not raise our boys in Detroit."

He said, "That's fine. I'm leaving." I was in such shock; it was so hard to believe what I was hearing.

I said to him, "Would you leave us for a year?"

He said, "Yes."

I said, "Would you leave us for two years?"

He replied, "Yes. Whatever it takes!" In my mind I was thinking, *Whatever it takes? What does that mean?*

I asked one more time, "Would you leave us for five years?"

He sternly replied, "Yes! Whatever it takes!" He then turned and walked out of the bedroom where we were having the discussion.

I had no clue at the time that what I was saying was prophetic. Exactly five years to the day he was gone and did not come back.

After two months passed, and he had not even tried to contact us or come home, I called him. I said to him, "You have abandoned us!" My husband was abandoned at birth and adopted out. His biological father basically was not there for him. He now in turn was abandoning us. Scripture says the sins of the father are unto the third and fourth generation.

When I spoke this truth to him, he just said, "Huh, yeah, I guess I can see that." That was it. The conversation was over.

I don't know how I made it through the next five years. He came home very little, maybe two to three times a year.

I was very busy raising the sons, taking care of the home, and volunteering full time in the ministry of Operation Christmas Child. All those things helped me to just keep going and to keep my eyes fully on the Lord.

I began to realize there was nothing left in our marriage. It was such a hard time in my life going through this. At the same time, God showed up so *big* in my life. He was always there for me providing, protecting, and blessing me and the boys. I learned in those five years to go to Him for everything. Big or small no matter, He wanted to hear it all. I grew in my faith and intimacy with Him.

I had an encounter with the Lord at church shortly after my husband left for Detroit. I was at church standing in the pew with three of my sons standing to my right. Ironically, they were in exact birth order, oldest to youngest. We were in worship at the time. I felt the presence of the Lord come and stand right next to me on my left. It was one of those moments where it is so real I didn't dare look over. I *knew* it was Him!

He spoke and said, "I am your husband and the Father of your sons." There was a huge relief that came over me. I knew I was not alone, and no matter what, He would take care of me and my sons!

I began to dread the weekends that my husband would come home. When he walked through the door, so did all the demonic activity and foolish behavior. We would go from peace and harmony in the house to chaos and division. I just kept asking the Lord, "How long, oh Lord, how long?"

Divorce was not an option for me. It was not in my vocabulary! I would stay committed no matter what. I had no clue God had other plans.

Chapter 6

DIVORCE

It was the end of March 2013. I was driving alone on my way to Orlando, Florida, for an Operation Christmas Child Connect Conference. I cried out to the Lord about my marriage all the way down. I said, "You have to step in and do something because I can't do it anymore. Something has to change before I get back. I also want to remind You divorce is not an option." At this point, I had been married for twenty-nine years.

The drive to Florida took two days. Late in the afternoon of the second day, I arrived at the condo of one of my dear friends, Sarah. I had planned to stay with her for two days before going to the conference. The day I arrived was Good Friday, so she and I went to church service that night.

Before entering the church, I prayed to the Lord, "Please speak to me through the sermon. Please give me something to know that you heard my desperate cry for help in my marriage."

When the sermon was over, I was disappointed because I felt like I had not received anything from Him. The preacher said, "Let me close in prayer." As I closed my eyes for prayer, I instantly had a vision. I saw in front of me a very bright white puffy cloud, and in the middle of the cloud was the word "TRUTH" in black lettering. So it stood out very well. As I was seeing this vision, the pastor had prayed out at that moment, "Father, illuminate the truth to your people."

I was so excited! He did speak to me! What did this mean? What was He saying to me? I didn't know, but He is a good communicator, and I knew He would show me.

As we left the church, I shared this with my friend. When we got in the car, I said to her, "I want to lift this up in prayer right now to Him."

I believe it is so important when we feel that God has spoken to us that we acknowledge Him first and then give back to Him what He is saying. That way, we can't control it. It is back in His hands to do what He wants to do with it. So I did just that. I asked Him, "What are you saying to me and what does this mean, illuminate the truth?"

He answered me that night in a dream. In the dream, I was standing just inside the front door of my home. My husband came through the front door very angry. I said to him, "What is wrong? What is the matter?"

He answered, "I had to tell my mom something she didn't like, and she got very mad at me." He started to walk away from me, and I grabbed his shoulder and swung him around.

I said to him, "You know you are going to have to stand up to her and tell her the truth!" He walked away very angry at me. That was the end of the dream.

When I shared it with my friend the next morning, she asked, "What do you think it means?"

I said, "He never 'left' his mother when we got married. He never did what the Bible says you are to do as a man, which is to leave your father and mother and cleave to your wife. We have always had a third person in our marriage. It has been just one of the many huge problems that exist. My husband flat out told me one time I will hurt you before I hurt my mother. So I believe God has illuminated the truth to me like I had prayed and asked for." I felt the Lord was showing me my husband was not willing to leave his mother and cleave to his wife through the dream.

I knew He was preparing me for an even greater illumination. He was beginning to answer my cry for help in the marriage. I wondered what would come next.

The next morning, my conversation with Sarah steered toward my marriage. Sarah had prayed with me for years about my marriage. Numerous times she had said, "I feel you need to leave and get out of this abusive situation." I refused to listen to her, believing God would step in and rescue it. I kept reminding her I had made a covenant before God. I would not break it!

Suddenly, in a very loud stern voice, which I had *never* heard her speak before, she began to speak forth the truth! She said, "Enough! No more! I don't want you to speak his name again. You need to get out! He is controlling your every thought! No more! You need to get out! I don't want to talk about this anymore!" When she was done speaking, she immediately began to apologize. "I don't know what came over me. I am so sorry for talking that way. I have never spoken to anyone that way before."

I said, "Absolutely not. Don't apologize. You did nothing wrong. I knew it wasn't you. I knew it was the Holy Spirit that took over. What you said is true. It came from Him, and I have to listen to it."

She was right. Finally, I was ready to listen and do what He was saying about my marriage. It was now clear to me that I had made an idol of my marriage. I needed to divorce my husband. I knew this was the second "illumination of truth" that He brought forth.

Later that same day, I checked into the hotel where the OCC conference was being held. I brought all my things to the room. Once I was settled in, I received a text from one of my team members that she had just landed and would be taking the next shuttle out to the motel. She figured fifteen minutes, and she would be there. I went to the outside lobby to wait for her.

I found a seat on one end of a couch. There was a man sitting on the other end of the couch. I sat down and said, "Hello. Are you here for the OCC conference?"

He said, "No." He then asked, "What is that?" I explained the ministry to him. I can be very descriptive and very enthusiastic about the ministry. He responded with "Wow, it sounds like you are really into the ministry, but I have to say you are not walking the talk." Those words pierced to my soul. I knew what he meant. I love and serve the Lord in every area of my life except my marriage. I wanted to hold it tight and hang on till God moved in to change it. Something was beginning to break that old thinking off of me. God was moving in a way I had not expected or anticipated.

This stranger began to speak about my husband's life in great detail. I had never met this man before. He said, "You know this is a divine appointment?" He told me things that my husband had said and done that he should have no way of knowing. He shared that my husband had cheated on me. "You thought you were protecting the kids by staying, but in fact, it had hurt them." He shared out loud even the thoughts I was having while sitting there listening to all of this. The bottom line of the conversation was him saying "Get out! No more! God created you for so much more."

I said, "I can't. I can't. I don't know how I will make it."

At that point, I realized my friend should have arrived forty-five minutes ago. We had been in conversation that long, and I didn't even realize it. I didn't understand where she was.

He said to me, "I want to finish this conversation over dessert. Let's go into one of the restaurants and finish this conversation over dessert."

I told him, "I have to wait for my friend because I have her room key."

He said, "Go inside, give her key to the concierge, then text your friend and let her know where her key is." So I got up and did what he said.

After doing that, I turned around and went back outside, and he was gone—nowhere to be found. I never saw him again. It was at that moment I knew I had been with an angel. This was now the third "illumination of the truth." Same message.

As I walked through the door, the friend I had been waiting for was stepping off the airport shuttle. She looked at me and said, "You are not going to believe what I've been through to get here. I should have been here forty-five minutes ago." I knew why she had been so delayed. God had set up a divine appointment to bring me His message. Nothing was going to interrupt it.

On our walk up to the room together, I told her about the encounter I had with what I know to be a real live angel. I shared with her that was why she was so delayed in getting to the motel. After I had shared everything with her, I got up to use the restroom.

When I came back out, she said, "I have a word for you, but I don't want to give it to you. It's not good."

I said, "Let it out. Nothing can be worse than what the angel just said to me."

She said, "The Lord told me to tell you, you are a battered wife."

For the first time I saw what she was saying, and I knew it was true. I just never wanted to admit it. I just kept hoping, trying, and believing it was all going to work out, and I could stay in my marriage. This was now the fourth "illumination" from Him.

At that moment, I was experiencing fear trying to take me over. I knew what the Lord was saying and what I needed to do, but I was so scared. At that exact moment, I heard a text ding on my phone. The phone was in my hand. So I looked down at it, and I saw the scripture John 14:27 (NASB), "Peace I leave with you; My peace I give you; not as the world gives, do I give to you. Let not your heart be troubled nor let it be fearful."

It was from my best friend Anna back in Michigan. She had no idea what was going on or what I was experiencing. She told me later she just felt impressed to send that verse at that time. Amazing! It literally took the fear that I was experiencing in that moment away!

I went on to attend the weeklong conference. My thoughts kept returning to "I cannot divorce him." It was so hard to concentrate on the conference and why I was there. I'm not sure how I made it through the week, but I did.

Anna had made arrangements to fly down on Saturday to attend the culminating concert at the end of the conference and then accompany me on my drive back home.

I had no idea the day I left for this conference what I would encounter there, but God did. He arranged for my best friend to be there for me in the worst thing that was about to happen to me in my life. I was heading for a divorce, the very thing I said I would never do.

The morning after the concert, we began our journey home. While I was driving, I shared with her the details of my week. I told her about the encounters I had had with my friend and the angel. I told her about the dreams and about my prayers to God, pleading with Him to lead me. By the time we stopped for the night, I was exhausted. I was anxious, scared, and physically drained. I collapsed on the bed and began to sob. I said to my friend, "What am I going to do?"

She replied, "I don't know, but God knows. Let's just give it to Him." She said a short prayer and ended with "God, you speak to Dianna in dreams. Please give her a dream tonight."

I had just that, a dream. In the dream, I was sitting on a couch in the inside lobby of the hotel I had just stayed at for the conference. My friend Sarah, who had sternly spoken to me, was sitting in a chair beside me. I heard the revolving front door of the motel go around. So I knew someone just entered the motel. When I looked up, I saw a man walking toward us. I recognized him as the one I had encountered on the couch, coming through the door. He was carrying two small personal-size pizza boxes on top and two medium sized underneath. The boxes were closed, but I knew the top two were pizzas. I knew the bottom two were dessert pizzas. I said to him as he was coming toward me, "I didn't order them. How did you know I was here?" The dream ended.

I felt the Lord gave me the interpretation. The man was the angel I encountered before. He, along with my friend Sarah, delivered two personal messages at the Hilton Hotel to me. If I would obey the two messages given, the end results would be sweet. Indicating the two dessert pizzas on the bottom, I would also receive a double portion, two dessert pizzas. I also realized I had just finished the conversation with the angel over dessert.

How could I deny what this was saying to me? This was now the fifth "illumination" of truth from Him. It was from that moment on that I set my face like a flint to obey what He was telling me I needed to do. I would start as soon as I arrived home. The first thing I did when I got home was to find a lawyer. I knew I wanted one who was a believer. I had him start the paperwork, but I also felt led to give one last opportunity for my husband to change.

So the next weekend that he came home from Detroit, I communicated with him that I wanted to see a change in him and toward our marriage, or I would be taking steps toward leaving. He was leaving that day to go back to Detroit. I told him I would give him until the following night to think about it, and I would be calling him the night after that for an answer. I needed to hear from him "Yes, I am willing to change to stay in the marriage." I called the next night, and there was no change.

So the night before I would hand in the papers, I asked the Lord to confirm what I was doing. This action would change my life forever, and I needed to know that He was still guiding me to get a divorce.

I had a dream that night. I was back home where I grew up. I was asleep along with everyone else in the house. When I woke up and looked out the window, I saw wind carrying debris past the window. I got up and went to the back door of the house and opened it. I saw a huge fireball rolling over the tops of the trees coming at me very swiftly. I shut the door. I began running through the house waking everyone up to get out. My son, grandson, brother, and mom met with me in the dining room. I said, "Run!" The dream ended.

I felt the Lord showed me judgment was about to fall. I must take the family and run, like Lot, or the judgment would fall on us all. By leaving, I would not only save myself but the extended family as well. This dream was confirmation that I was obeying the will of God. The story of Lot can be found in Genesis 18–19.

I continued to ponder these things in my heart as I went to the refrigerator the next morning. I retrieved two eggs to prepare my breakfast. When I cracked open the first egg, two yolks appeared! I was instantly reminded by Him of the double-portion promise. The odds of getting a double yoke are one in one thousand.

That was the morning I filed the divorce paperwork.

From that moment on, I felt like I was in a protective bubble. Job 1:10 (NASB) says, "Hast Thou not made a hedge about him and his house and all that he has, on every side?" It was there all the way through the divorce. There were no words or actions of harm that could break through that bubble. It was like nothing I've ever experienced before.

I had gone to a doctor's appointment that morning, and I pulled up to the office and parked my car. When I looked out my passenger side window, I saw an old railroad track that was no longer in use. It came right up to my parking spot and stopped. When I turned and looked out my left window, the track was gone where they had pulled it up. It was now the parking lot. The Lord spoke to me and said, "You are no longer on that old track, and you are now starting on a new one."

I have found during the hardest, most excruciating times, He manifests His presence the most. Although I hate hard times, I love His presence more. It is true that He will never leave you, nor forsake you. He is in every situation, even when you can't see or feel Him.

Early in the divorce process, I had a vision one morning during my prayer time. I saw the Lord inside my body standing by my heart. I realized what He was showing me. He was guarding my heart as I walked through this process of divorce.

At this point in my life, I'm looking at total destitution. I could end up with no home, no car, and an eight-dollar-an-hour part-time job. I only have a high school education. I stayed home and raised our four sons. I was fifty years old with twenty-nine years of dedication to a marriage that was ending. I was asking myself, *What will I do? How will I ever survive this?* Somehow deep inside me, I knew I would not just survive, but I would thrive in the end! I knew that didn't come from me but from Him!

Chapter 7

ONE STEP AT A TIME

I continued to share my divorce process experiences and my heart with Sarah. She was my prayer warrior. One day as I was speaking with her over the phone, she said to me, "Let's pray and take it before the Lord."

While she was praying, she had a vision. In the vision, she saw me on a path. The Lord was in front of me and was at my back. The path was very bright. She could only see the path right in front of me. She could not see a way out. She said, "The path you are on is from Him. He made the path. It is not crooked. It is straight. It is strong. It will not crumble under you. It is not rocky, so it will not hurt your feet. It is not icy, so you will not slip and fall. It is His pathway. Follow it and obey." I was seeing her describe how I was feeling from being in that bubble. That was the close protection I was receiving daily. It was incredible! I never wanted it to end. I knew this vision was from the Lord. I grabbed ahold of it.

When things would get really hard, I went back to the vision and what He had promised me. It sustained me many times. It gave me the confidence to move ahead knowing He was right there with me. He was guiding me and keeping me right where I needed to be.

When I started the divorce process, I was working part-time at a resale store as an assistant manager, making just eight dollars an hour. I had no savings. At that time in the marriage, I was only given enough money for food and gas. I knew that I had no way of making it through the divorce financially. I also knew once I was on my own, I would have to fully rely on God for everything. So began the greatest journey of faith yet in my life.

The miracles started happening. The first one was tires for a car I didn't even own yet. My part-time job was assistant manager at a resale sale store owned by the local Christian school. I was getting ready to close the store when a donation came to the back door. These were eight sixteen-inch tires. We had never been given a donation of tires before. We just don't take them. I said to the man, "We don't take tires here."

He said to me, "These are very expensive winter and all-season tires, and they are in good shape."

So I went to my manager and asked him, "Do you want to accept these tires?"

He said, "Take them. We will try to sell them online."

The minute I shut the door after taking in the tires, a thought came. *Lord, are these tires for the car you're going to get for me?* He has done similar things like that before with me.

That night when I got home I thought, *I better start looking for a car.* I went on Craigslist, and the first car I found was a 1999 Pontiac Bonneville. It only had 65,000 miles on it. The asking price was two thousand dollars. I called and went out to look at it that night.

On the way out I said, "God, if the tires that we just took in at the store will fit this car I'm going to buy it because I will know this is you." I brought all the cash I had, two hundred dollars at the time. Not only did the tires fit the car, the seller was willing to accept my two-hundred-dollar down payment and allow me to return with the balance of $1,800 the next day to pick up the car. I did not have cash at home, and I wasn't sure where I would get it.

I went home and called my mom and dad who live an hour north of my hometown. My sister, who also lives in Traverse City, happened to be there visiting my parents. My parents gave my sister the money I needed, and the cash was in my hand that night! I bought the car first thing in the morning.

Buying that car seemed to come with such ease. I became certain of two things. First, God had done it. I had nothing to do with it. And second, this was how He was going to take care of me. The very next morning when I went to work, I told my manager that I had bought a car, and the tires we had taken in the day before would fit the car. So I said to him, "I would like to buy both sets of tires."

He said, "Take them home. They are yours!"

I was shocked and so thankful! The next thing was, where will I live?

I did not know what was going to happen to the house that we both owned. I was hoping to get the house, but of course, if I got the house, I would get the debt as well. I had no way of making the payment. If I had to pay him half of the value of the house, there was *no way* I could do that. I would have to just wait and see what the outcome would be.

I did not want to fight for anything. I only wanted freedom from the situation I found myself in. There are laws in place to make decisions in matters like this. I did not need to fight. The Lord fought for me. He is also the ultimate judge. I had a vision in the family courtroom to show me this.

In the courtroom was myself and my husband at the time. We were waiting for the judge to come out. In the vision, I saw to my right rows of angels standing at attention looking to the judge's chair. I saw the Lord come out from a back room and stand behind the judge's chair. I knew that He was *the* judge and that He would have the final word in this decision. I knew He was looking at myself and my husband. He was looking into our hearts and judging our motives. The angels standing to my right were waiting and watching for orders from Him to go do His bidding on our behalf. When I left the courtroom that day, I *knew* God, in every and all situations, is the judge with the final word.

Throughout the divorce process, God set up things that happened in my favor, and I had nothing to do with it. Nor did my lawyer. His hand was visible throughout the six-month ordeal.

Something incredible happened the day my divorce became final. I woke up and saw two visions that played over and over again in my mind all day.

In the first one, I was standing in a jail cell, and the door was all the way open. I heard the Lord speak to me, "You are free." I saw myself walking through the door. I felt the Lord show me that day He had set me free from the prison I had been in.

This is what I saw in the second one. It was a beautiful sunny day outside, and in front of me was a big round table. On the table was a very large book. It was about three-fourths of the way open. I saw a huge hand come down out of the sky and turn the next page. I knew that page was the beginning of a new chapter. The book was my life story. I was fifty at the time of the divorce. That is about three-fourths of my life. I felt the Lord showed me He was in control of my life. He was orchestrating the next chapter, and like the sunny day, it would be beautiful.

The next morning, my friend Pam called me and told me she was listening to someone on the radio who had just gone through a divorce. She made the statement that divorce was not her story, only a chapter in the book. She also said that she kept a journal, and the day she was divorced, she had started a new journal. She had just filled her last one. My friend did not know of my vision about the book. I too keep a journal and just started a new journal the day after my divorce. God was really speaking to me. He was saying you will be starting out fresh and the best is yet to come!

In the divorce settlement, I received alimony for four and a half years and child support for my minor son. I got the house with a mortgage debt of about $138,000. I was not required to pay my husband his share of equity. I did not receive any retirement or cash. My monthly expenses would be $2,700. I would have no health insurance, and I was still working part time at eight dollars an hour.

I had to step down and leave the ministry of Operation Christmas Child, but the Lord told me I would step back in when the time was right. He would open that door again.

I asked the Lord, "How will I ever pay my bills alone?" Somehow I knew He would continue to be faithful to direct me. I want to say it again; there was nothing in and of myself that I could do to make it. I had to live by faith and trust Him alone. As long as I kept my eyes on Him, I was okay. The divorce became final on October 18, 2013, and winter was just around the corner.

---- Chapter 8 ----

ONE PROVISION AT A TIME

With each step I took by His guidance, a wonderful provision would follow. My friends knew I didn't have the money for heating, so they called and told me they were bringing me a pallet of wood pellets for my pellet stove. When they arrived, they had two pallets of pellets. They commented to me, "Two pallets, double portion!" God was reminding me of His double-portion promise He had made to me.

Things began to happen so fast. I began to pick up jobs like cleaning, taking care of the elderly, landscaping, and painting, anything to earn extra money so I could pay the bills. It was extremely hard as I was working seven days a week from eight to eight most days with no break.

Just a few days after the divorce, I had a lightning strike very close to the house. Within a day or two, I had two small motors quit from the strike. One was my pellet stove fan, and the other one was the fan on my gas hot water heater. My insurance paid all but my five-hundred-dollar deductible. God covered me there by my sister finding out, and she paid part of it. An unexpected check came in the mail for the rest of it.

The gentleman who fixed my pellet stove fan said that I was very fortunate from the strike because the life expectancy for those motors is five years. It had been five years, so it was due to go out anyway. God again looked out for me and the double portion.

The home that I own and live in is 3,700 square feet. The main level is 1,500. The basement is 1,500. The one-and-a-half-story house upstairs is 700 square feet. The basement is partially finished off, and the Cape was only to the studs. I was living alone in the house. The Lord began to impress on me to get the basement finished off. It would have a full kitchen, dining, living room, bathroom, two bedrooms, with a washer and dryer.

I had no idea financially how to pay for it. I had to totally step out in faith and just do it. I prayed and looked to Him. I went and bought kitchen cabinets, a toilet, and kitchen sink at a resale shop. A stove and microwave came into my resale shop, and I bought the fridge and stack washer and dryer from Craigslist. I cannot even tell you how I got this all done. I only know when He tells you to do something, just step out and do it, and He will supply. I finished the basement.

On February 1, 2015, I had two ladies from my church move into the basement and start paying $250 each a month in rent. I found God bringing me what I needed when I needed it and how I needed it!

I also have a thirty-by-forty pole barn on my property. I cleared it out because I surely didn't need it, and I had a building contractor move in. I started getting $300 a month rent on that.

While my car was parked at work during the winter, some snow and ice fell off the roof of the building and broke my driver-side mirror off. I was so disappointed and upset because I really didn't have the money to fix it. Once again, God showed up and took care of it.

The morning after the mirror was fixed, I pulled up at work and parked my car. I happened to look in my new mirror before I got out. When I looked at the mirror, I heard the Lord speak, "Now, no looking back." I knew what He meant.

It had been almost one year since the divorce, and I had spent much time looking back. I kept asking myself if there was anything I could have done to prevent this. I had spent time beating myself up, and the Lord was saying to me, "No more." It was time to move forward; no more looking back.

From that incident, I felt the Lord encourage me with this scripture, "Do not call to mind the former things, or ponder things of the past. Behold, I will do something new, now it will spring forth; will you not be aware of it" (Is 43:18–19 NASB)?

The next hurdle that was before me was to refinance the house. I was given the house along with the debt of $138,000 in the divorce. I had one year from the divorce to refinance and take my former husband's name off. If I couldn't, I would have to sell the house. I would get all the proceeds from the house, but the Lord had clearly shown me over and over I was not to sell. I was to keep the house. I consulted every lending institution out there, and no one would carry the loan for me.

My credit was just shy of the highest score you can get. The equity was well over a hundred thousand. It was my debt-to-income ratio that was not good. My income at that time was mostly from self-employment, and in order to use that income, I had to produce two years tax return to prove that income. I didn't even have one year.

So I went before the Lord, and I said, "I know You told me not to sell, but I have done all I can do, and I still cannot get a loan. I will have to sell. If You want me to keep it, You will have to step in and do it." Almost a year had passed, and I only had a few days left to refinance. So He would have to do it in a couple of days. He did just that.

Someone I know heard of my situation and stepped in and paid my house off *interest free*! My mortgage was now paid off, and I had a promissory note. I have to say this was the biggest miracle God had done for me yet. It was just absolutely incredible.

I now began to cry out to the Lord for something different for my work. As I said before, I was working seven days a week. Most days, it was eight in the morning to eight at night. Most of them were cleaning jobs that are very physical, and at the time, I was fifty. After a full year of this, I was worn-out and couldn't imagine having to do this until I retired. *Lord, what do You have for me next?*

What came next was a wonderful surprise. My manager at the store came to me and said, "I'm taking another job, so I will be leaving, and I'm going to recommend you as the next manager."

I was so excited God heard my prayer and answered it! I would be getting $30,000 a year and health insurance! I could quit all the other jobs and just have this one! God is so good to me!

What a blessing my new job was. I was able to relax and enjoy life a little more as I could see myself getting ahead a little with bills. I just felt all the pressure lift off.

We held a going-away party for my manager. At the party one, of my volunteers at the store came up to me and pulled me close and whispered to me, "This is only a stepping-stone for where God is going to be taking you next. You will not be in this job for very long." I was shocked, but I knew it was God.

I was in that position for a little over a year. I had never been a manager before, so I had a lot to learn. Working with people can be challenging. What I learned was to be humble, open for correction, and have a willingness to learn. These practices will not fail you. They will only grow you into a good leader.

As I told you earlier, the upstairs in my home was only finished to the studs. The Lord began to impress with urgency to finish the cape upstairs. Well, I thought that was silly. Why do I need to do that? There's only me. I already have 1,500 square feet to myself. I didn't have the money or the time, but once again, I knew all I had to do was listen and obey, and He would be the one responsible for doing it.

It's such an adventure with God when He tells you to do something as you step out and trust and believe He meets you there. He just started miraculously bringing the provision, the money, building materials, and labor. It just all showed up just when I needed it. He is amazing and faithful!

In the midst of this project, my thoughts returned to my good friend and volunteer at the store. I remembered her saying "This is only a stepping-stone. You won't be in this position long." I said, "Lord, does this have anything to do with You directing me to finishing off the cape? What are you up to? What is coming down the pipe?"

Chapter 9

THE STEPPING-STONE

The construction project upstairs was going along really well with Him supplying what I needed when I needed it. When it was done, it would consist of a bedroom, full bathroom, and a nice big sitting (prayer) room. The project was about three-quarters of the way done when I began feeling another prompting from the Lord. I felt Him saying it was time to leave my job and go to another one.

When I feel a prompting from the Lord, I first acknowledge Him and say, "Lord, I feel you are speaking to me." Then I begin taking steps toward what He is saying to me. I had no other job in mind. I had no idea where I would go. So as the promptings would come, I just kept saying to the Lord, "Okay, I hear You. I'm ready. I will do it, but I can't leave my job without another job in place." To me, that would not make sense. I actually felt it would be wrong to leave a job when I didn't have a job to go to. At that time, my monthly bills were about $2,700 a month.

Around this time, my church's Traverse Life Center Director, Megan, had decided to start a resale store to fund this center. Megan was coming to me to get advice about starting the store. She and I would have talks, and we would pray for God's direction and wisdom to begin the store.

Megan shared her ideas of what she wanted it to look like and the purpose of it. They were exactly the same as my purpose and reason for starting a resale store for Operation Christmas Child, which was Unlimited Hidden Treasures. So we both thought that was interesting how there was that connection. When she began coming to me, I somehow felt we would be connected through this resale store she wanted to start.

It was then that she shared with me she would like me to manage the store once it was up and running. She thought it would be about six or seven months out before that would happen. She could not officially ask me to manage it until it was up and running and producing the money to be able to pay my wage as manager. So for months, we were just in and out of conversation about this store and me possibly managing it.

During this same time, I was having a problem with my garage service door. I would go through the door and shut it, but it would not stay shut. No matter how many times I shut it, it would pop back open. I'm not very good at fixing things that involve construction or using power tools, so I continued to ignore it.

One morning, as I was walking through the service door on my way to work, I felt a strong prompting from the Lord that I was to actually quit my job that day. I continued to ignore this prompting because I didn't have a job to go to. I went through the service door of the garage and shut it. I got into my car to leave. I looked up, and I could see that the door had popped back open again. I got out of my car, and I was very upset. I started toward the service door to shut it. I spoke out loud, "God, I am so sick of this door! What is the problem?" I felt His presence come very strongly. It actually was so strong it scared me. I stopped immediately and said, "Lord, what is it?"

He said to me, "You are trying to shut a door that I want open. You are to quit your job today."

A chill of fear went down through me, and I said, "Lord, I have felt your promptings. I have acknowledged You, but I can't do what you're telling me to do because I don't have a job to replace it!"

He spoke very strongly and said, "You must quit your job today!"

I said, "Okay, Lord, I will do that, and I will trust you with the rest." I shut the service door.

I knew this was a *test*. He wanted me to step out into the unknown and just *trust* Him alone! It was perhaps the greatest faith test yet before me. No matter the level of fear, I was determined to move forward in what He was telling me to do. But sadly, my first go-to was "I have to figure this out."

I got into my car, and the first thing I did was call my mom. I said, "Mom, I don't understand. God has been telling me to leave my job, and I don't feel it's right because I don't have another job in its place. It doesn't make sense, but He just said to me very clearly this morning I am to quit my job today."

My mom replied, "Dianna, He wants you to leave your job, and you need to do that and just trust Him."

I knew she was right, but when I got off the phone, I immediately texted my friends who had given me work before to see if they would have work for me again. So here I was trying to figure it out again and take it upon myself to find work. I texted them and said, "Please, can we talk tonight when you guys get home?" These were the two ladies who lived in my basement. I had worked for both of them before I took the job I was in now.

When I got to work and went inside the back door, I was all alone. I called Megan and told her what had happened that morning and that God was telling me to quit my job that day. I told her I was very scared, and I didn't know what I was going to do. I asked her if there was any way that the store was ready to take me on in a paid position as manager.

Her response back to me was "No, I can't do that."

I said to her, "I understand. I am operating out of fear, and I just need to trust the Lord in this situation." I hung up the phone.

As I stood there all alone in the back room of the store, I cried out very loudly, "Lord, what are you doing to me? I am so scared! What am I to do?" Immediately, I had a vision, and it's one of those visions where I am seeing, hearing, and feeling it all at the same time. It was happening literally all around me.

I was standing on the bow of a ship that was out in the sea in a raging storm. I could hear the thunder and crashing of waves all around me. I heard a voice say, "Who has angered the gods?" I knew that it was me. I had heard from the Lord, and I was afraid to do what He was telling me to do. And I was running from it, just like

Jonah. I was experiencing what Jonah did when he disobeyed the Lord. The story of Jonah can be found in the Old Testament book titled Jonah.

I fell to my knees, and I said, "Oh, God, forgive me. I am so sorry. Today I will put my notice in and quit my job. I will trust you and not try to figure out a job."

One of the friends whom I had texted earlier to ask about a job decided to call me about three hours later. She wanted to find out what was going on. When she called me, I was in my car driving to meet someone for lunch. It was July Fourth weekend, and the Blue Angels were in town performing.

She asked me, "What is going on? Why do we need to talk tonight?"

I told her the whole story about the door and that the Lord told me I needed to quit my job that day. I said, "I am so scared, and I don't want to do it. Just a few hours ago, I had a vision, and from that vision, I am determined in my heart to not be afraid and just trust Him for a job. The reason I texted you about a meeting tonight was to ask you if you have any work for me. But I am no longer going to do that." At that moment, I looked up in the air, and in front of me were the Blue Angels. They were in formation crossing the sky, practicing for their show the next day. I said out loud, "The angels are in the air. They are going before me!" When I spoke that, and I heard it with my ears, I knew the Lord was speaking to me. What I saw was He had already dispatched the angels to go to work on my behalf to bring me whatever I needed. I said to my friend, "Did you just hear what I said?"

She said, "Yes, I did!"

I said, "God is going to take care of this. I trust Him!" I hung up the phone with her and continued on my way to meet my friend for lunch.

When our lunch was over I was prompted to stop and see another friend along my way home. I stopped to see her, and she could see on my face something was troubling me. I came in and sat down and began to share with her everything that had happened that morning.

Before I could finish sharing, she jumped up and ran to her bedroom and said, "Just a minute. I need to go do something." When she came back, she handed me a check for five thousand dollars. She said, "Is this enough to get you by until you get a job?"

I was so blown away! I dropped to my knees and just started crying and saying, "God, why didn't I just believe You. Why didn't I just believe You! Look at what You had planned and already in the works before I even said yes. I will quit my job." That night, I went home and emailed my two-week notice from my job.

Within a few days, Megan called me and offered me the job at the new thrift store. She said to me, "The board agreed that it would be okay to go ahead and hire you as the manager!" The name of the store is Restored Treasures.

There were two things that God did here for me. First, my faith grew immensely. I could see and understand that He is always working behind the scenes even when I can't see it. He has me covered no matter what. He *will* take care of me.

Secondly, from the time of the divorce, I had been working seven days a week. I had my part-time job, cleaning, landscaping, and taking care of the elderly all at once. From there, I went into the manager's position of the store that was six days a week. I was working about sixty to seventy hours. I was desperate for a break, for a little vacation. I had asked the Lord when He was prompting me to leave my job for a little vacation. I knew it was impossible, but I would love to have a month off with a little vacation and the money to do it.

That is exactly what He gave me. I had exactly thirty days off between jobs. I was able to take a little vacation. I had the money to pay all my bills during that time and pay for the vacation with the five thousand dollars He had given me. He is so amazing and faithful!

This new job that I would step into as a manager also allowed me to go down to part time. I would be working three days a week and one Saturday a month. This was an answer to my prayer. You ask how I could go down to part-time financially? Well, let me tell you.

You see, in the middle of the building project and job change, something else was happening simultaneously. I was being led by the Lord to take in Chinese high school students for the upcoming school year. This would be perhaps the biggest of all the transitions taking place in my life. This one needs a chapter all on its own.

Chapter 10

BECOMING A MOM AGAIN AT 52

The prompting came for the students when I had several of them come to the store and volunteer to fulfill their community hours requirement. As I was working side by side with them, I really enjoyed being with them. I had feelings rise up that I would like to be a host mom for these students. I recognized those feelings were not coming from me but from Him. Psalm 37:4 (NASB) says, "Delight yourself in the Lord; and He will give you the desires of your heart."

He wanted me to take some Chinese students in for that coming school year. I said, "Lord, how can I do this? How will this ever work? How will I ever have time for the students working as many hours as I am?" I had no idea at the time the job change would allow me to only have to work part time. This would allow me the time to be with and take care of them. This transition of jobs would take place before I even got them! But again, I did not know that at the time.

All of this was happening at the same time, and it wasn't all shown to me while I was in it. I did not see or understand it until it was all over and in place. It requires so much faith as you walk through things like this. Most of the time when God is moving and speaking, you only get a part of the full picture. I believe He does it that way with me because otherwise, I would try to control it. He just wants me to listen, hear, obey, and trust Him completely with it all.

With the stipend that I would receive for the students, my part-time job, rent from my basement, and rent from my pole barn, there would be enough for me to live on. I would even be able to start saving a little bit each month!

It was then that it hit me; so this is why the prompting and urgency to get the upstairs finished off. It was the beginning of March when He told me to get started on the project. The students would arrive at the end of August. It was all coming together. It was all adding up and making sense now. The Chinese students would be housed on the main floor of the house, and I would be upstairs by myself. I could see His plan unfolding perfectly.

I would just like to add here that I was not in charge of any of this. None of this was coming from me. I have learned to give Him complete control of everything. I don't have to know or figure anything out. My role is to listen, hear, trust, and obey. He does all the rest. Psalm 18:30 (NASB) says, "As for God, His way is blameless."

Before I said yes to the Chinese students, I did ask the Lord to confirm this was what He wanted me to do. So the night before I said yes, I had a dream.

In the dream, there was a very large 747 passenger plane with red, white, and blue colors. It was sitting directly in front of me. There was a set of steps in front of me leading to the plane. As I entered into the dream, I heard "One, two, three, go!" I was lifted up and literally floating down the steps. I reached the plane first, and when I turned around, I saw a great number of Chinese boys standing there, looking at me smiling. I then woke up. There was my confirmation. I knew I was to take in the Chinese boys for the upcoming school year.

Two nights later, the Lord gave me another dream about this new transition that was coming.

In this dream, I was on a very familiar road that I travel a lot. As I was driving down the road, to my left appeared a new road veering off to the left. This was new, and I had not seen it before. I quickly turned onto that new road. As I was doing so, my mind was saying, *No, that's not the right way.* I have never gone that way before. Then I woke up.

I knew what it meant. This would be a new path that I have never traveled before, taking these boys in. I knew at this point I would be in disobedience if I didn't say yes.

—————— Chapter 11 ——————

THE FOUR *J*S

When I was told there were over forty students to choose from, I thought, *How will I ever decide which ones?* I took it to the Lord. I knew He would show me. The gentleman that I was working with, Judah, called and set up a time to meet with me to discuss which students I would get.

When he arrived, he told me that he had narrowed it down to ten boys to make it easier to pick from. At this point, because my dream had shown only Chinese boys, and I had raised four boys of my own, it made sense to choose boys.

The Chinese students pick American names for themselves before they arrive in the states. Judah pulled up the first student and said, "Let's start with John." He read me his profile.

I said, "Yes, I would like to have John." The next one he pulled was Jason. The moment he began to read his profile, the Lord spoke to me and said, "They all must begin with *J*." I just started laughing and said in my head, *Only you, God.* You see, my four sons all start with a *B*.

I said to Judah, "Do you have two more boys that start with *J*?"

He looked at me puzzled and said, "Well, I think I do, but why? I don't understand."

I said, "Well, I prayed about which ones to pick and trusted God to show me, and He did." I explained how I had four boys, and they all started with *B*. So when the Lord said they all need to start with a *J*, it made perfect sense. Of course, He would do that!

68

Looking through the files, Judah found only two more. So I chose John, Jason, Jake, and Joel. He didn't need to read me their profiles. I had my boys! God had chosen them! Just like I knew He would.

So it was all set up, and I knew this was what the Lord wanted me to do, but that didn't mean it was going to be easy. I just had a lot of concerns. What if they didn't like me? What if I didn't like them? What if I didn't even know what to do with them? What if the stipend was not enough to cover all expenses? What if? What ifs could go on forever. God brought me a very powerful assurance that all my "what-ifs" would be taken care of.

It came a few days after my "what if" rant. He sent a young man from my church to my home with a prophetic word for me. I did not know this twenty-year-old very well. So it seemed a little odd when he came knocking on my door one summer Sunday afternoon.

I had my family over for lunch. When he knocked on the door, I invited him to come in and eat lunch with us. He sat next to me at the table, and we began to engage in a conversation to catch up with our lives.

When he asked me what was going on in my life, I began to tell him the story of the four *J*s' coming.

He was amazed and very excited for me. He then spoke these words to me, "You know, whatever God calls you to, He will provide all you need to do it." I did know this, but I had forgotten it. Sometimes we need to recall what we know to be true about Him.

He stayed for a few minutes more after lunch, and before he left, he turned to me and said it again, "Remember whatever God calls you to, He will provide whatever you need to do it."

I thanked him and then walked him to the door and said, "Goodbye."

As I was shutting the door, I thought, *Lord, that was odd. Why did he come here?*

My kids looked at me and said out loud what I was thinking. "Mom, that was odd. Why did he come?"

The Lord answered me right away and said, "I sent him with a prophetic word to let you know I will provide all that you need for these boys coming!" Peace and assurance flooded me. I knew it was going to work out just fine.

I have found that when I experience something odd or bizarre, and it captures my attention, He usually wants to speak to me. So what I do is stop and say, "What is it? What are You saying?" Most of the time, He answers right away. If not, it might come later. If I hear nothing, then it is nothing. I do feel He speaks to me a lot through circumstances surrounding me at the time. The encounter I had with the young man from my church is an example of this.

My first day at Restored Treasures was August 16, and the students arrived on August 31. So I had only a few days to prepare and get ready for them. I was literally putting the finishing touches on the upstairs room where I would be sleeping. Perfect timing.

The day after they arrived, there appeared a double rainbow in the sky over my home. For me that was a major confirmation from the Lord. I had just stepped into both my new job and the hosting of the Chinese students. Both were out of obedience to what He had told me to do. The rainbow for me was a promise that He would be with me.

Before they came, I was worried about whether I would be able to really love them. So I cried out to the Lord for love for the boys. I know if love is present, the rest takes care of itself. He gave me a profound love like I have never experienced before. Yes, it was hard working part-time and taking care of the boys, but the joy, love, and adventure was so much greater!

I knew before they came that part of my hosting job would be teaching them. I had not anticipated how much I would learn from them. I was so blessed by their being here. The blessing spilled over into my family, over my kids, and grandkids.

The very first meal we ate together, I shared a few things with them. I told them that I had prayed for them before they even got here. I told them the process of how God had chosen them by name for me. I shared that I believed God brought them here for a purpose and a reason and that He loved them very much.

Out of the four boys, I connected the most with Joel. He was more open and willing to take the time to communicate with me. Right away I could see the Lord revealing Himself to Joel.

When the boys first arrived, I shared with them that God had handpicked them and brought them to my house. After about two weeks, Joel pulled me aside and said, "I need to talk to you alone. Do you remember when you said God picked us? Well, I know it is true. We are pure. The rest of the kids drink, smoke, swear, and they're doing things with girls."

He was crying and shaking, and I could see that the Lord was revealing Himself to Joel and bringing revelation. That moment was so powerful because for me, I was seeing what God told me would happen. All I could do was praise and thank Him for what He was doing in Joel's life. Joel could see, out of all the students that came, they were best suited for my home. As a nonbeliever, how could he see this other than God revealed it to him? What a precious way for God to do this.

The next encounter with God for Joel would be through sausage. Joel asked to have sausage with his breakfast every day. I explained to him that it was expensive, and I couldn't afford to buy it, so it would have to be something we would pray for. I explained how God was my provider, and when I didn't have the means for something, I would turn to Him to supply it. So we began praying for sausage.

The very next day, I was on my way to church with the four J's in the car with me. My phone rang, and when I answered it, I put it on speaker so my hands were free to drive.

My daughter-in-law said, "Hello, my mom is cleaning her freezer out, and she has six pounds of sausage she's trying to get rid of. Would you like it?" My heart skipped a beat, and I just began laughing. All the boys heard what God just did. He had answered our prayers. He will use anything to reveal Himself to us.

The Lord continued in different ways to reveal Himself to the boys. I wish I could say they all came to know the Lord as their Savior, but they didn't. I know, however, that seeds had been planted, and they will be watered by someone else.

The following school year, I received two new male students as the four *J*s moved on to college. That was a hard year as these new students came with many issues. The Lord helped me to navigate through it, and I was thankful for His help.

The following year, the program was cancelled by the school, so there would be no new students available for me to host. The Lord would have to provide financially through another avenue. *What's next, God?*

Chapter 12

LIFE ON THE EDGE!

When you are walking with the Holy Spirit, there is never a dull moment. I would call it a high adventure every day with Him.

Before the next school year started, I received a prompting from the Lord to go back to the vision of Unlimited Hidden Treasure. That was the nonprofit that I had created for funding packed shoeboxes for Operation Christmas Child. I knew it would mean I would have to quit the job I had just started and go start my own resale store.

The next morning, in my *Jesus Calling* devotion, the author said, "Be willing to go out on a limb for Jesus." Later that day when I was at Sam's Club shopping in the book aisle, the book *Jump* by Steve Harvey literally jumped out at me! The whole book is about you having to just step out and do things, or nothing will happen. You have to take a risk. Those who accomplish a lot have to let go of fear and just *jump*! This was reinforcing the promptings from the Lord that I needed to step into Unlimited Hidden Treasures.

That same day, the Lord also began prompting me to look to Him and trust Him by faith with my finances. I have always been a good steward of money and believe very strongly in living within a budget. For years, I had consistently followed the envelope method. My income was disbursed every month into envelopes labeled with the bill they would cover. The Lord was telling me that He would become my budget.

For me to hear this, it almost seemed wrong. It just couldn't be God asking me to do it. As time went on, I knew that it was Him. I knew I was to deposit all of the money that I had in envelopes into the bank. I knew I was not to look back. I knew I was not to budget for the bills or my needs. I was to fully walk in looking to Him for the provision. I was no longer looking at a budget.

In the past, I would argue and stall what He would ask me to do; I was not going to do that anymore. That day, I deposited all the money from my budget envelopes in the bank. I took that step of faith that I would no longer be operating on a budget. He was now my budget!

The very next day, I had pipes freeze in my bathroom on the second floor. They burst open, and water flooded from the second floor down to the first floor and then down to the basement. So all three floors had water damage. I knew immediately that I was being tested because I had just stepped out in faith with my finances. I have found when God calls you to do something big, and you obey, you will immediately be tested in that very thing.

What's amazing is that, that same morning, I had said to the Lord that I really needed new carpet for the main floor of the house. It was in bad shape, but I had no money to get new ones. So I had to turn to the Lord who is my provider, Jehovah Jireh. When the pipes burst, I got new carpet. So in a sense, you could say He answered my prayer that day. It was quite amazing!

About a month had passed since the Lord had prompted me to get back into Unlimited Hidden Treasures. I had done nothing about it, mainly because it would require going out and looking for a building to start a resale store. I didn't have the time or money to do that. It was something utterly impossible.

One morning as I walked into the kitchen to prepare my break-fast, my eyes landed on a magnet hanging on the refrigerator door. It is one I made years ago, and a Bible verse was printed on it. The scripture is Proverbs 3:5–6 (NASB), "Trust in the Lord with all your heart and do not lean on your own understanding. In all your ways acknowledge Him, and He will make your paths straight." I had added the word "FLY" as a reminder that the woman who chooses to trust in the Lord will "fly" with Him. Well, the word *fly* came right out into my face. I knew that the Lord was saying to me this morning you are to tell your manager that you are going to leave your job. It was time to begin the journey. It was time to start looking for a building to house the resale store for Unlimited Hidden Treasures. This was very scary for me, and I did not want to do it. Despite the fear, I knew from past experience if I obey, everything will be okay.

I shared with my manager, Megan, what the Lord had been showing me for over a month. I did not know exactly how things would develop, but I had to communicate to her that the Lord was directing me back to Unlimited Hidden Treasures.

She was very disappointed and did not want to see me go. She asked, "When would you be leaving?"

I said to her, "I don't know. Are you willing to just let this unfold and see what God is going to do?"

She said, "Absolutely. The longer you stay, the better for me. But I know you have to do what the Lord is telling you to do. I will be here for you and help you in any way that I can. I support you all the way!" I was amazed and so thankful how supportive she was.

That night, I was awakened at 11:56 p.m. I couldn't wait to get up in the morning to see what scripture He was giving me and what He was saying. I found Hebrews 11:5–6 (NASB).

> By faith Enoch was taken up so that he should
> not see death; and he was not found because God
> took him up; for he obtained the witness that
> before his being taken up he was pleasing to God.
> And without faith it is impossible to please Him.
> For he who comes to God must believe that He
> is, and that He is a rewarder of those who seek
> Him.

I felt the Lord was saying to me because I had taken that step of faith, that He was pleased with me.

Just a few days later, as I was walking in the mall by a shoe store, they had a big sign that said "STEP FORWARD." Those words jumped right out at me! I felt it was a confirmation from the Lord of what

I had just done. He is so good about confirming and reassuring me when I obey Him in a situation.

I want to encourage you with something that I have experienced again and again. When God is calling me to do something, no matter where I go, what I see, what I hear, it's all saying the same thing. It all points back to what He just told me to do. God will be very faithful about reinforcing what He said as you listen and obey. He is a very good communicator!

It was the next day after I had taken that step that He gave me a dream. It showed me that one of my dearest friends, Pam, was to partner with me in this endeavor. In response to the dream, I said to the Lord, "If this dream is of You, then I want her to call me with the same message." I didn't want it to come from me. I wanted it to come from her. That way, I would know that it was God doing it and not me.

Within a day, Pam called me from Arizona. She has a home near me in Michigan but spends several months in Arizona with her sister over the winter. She said to me that the Lord had spoken to her and told her that she was to partner with me in this new ministry! How amazing! I was so thankful that God was bringing someone alongside of me so I didn't have to walk this journey alone.

I began going out to look for buildings where I could start a resale store. It seemed like everywhere I went, the door shut. There was nothing opening up.

One morning while I was in my quiet time with Him, I heard the Lord say to me, "You will not be looking for a building. You'll be listening for my voice."

I said, "Okay, Lord, then that is what I will do. I will stop looking for a building, and I will just wait to hear from you."

A few days later, my manager, Megan, came to me and said, "I really feel the Lord was speaking to me that we should combine efforts. We already have a resale store established here. You told me that when you start your Unlimited Hidden Treasures you are going to be volunteering. You would be working but not taking a paycheck. So I would like to make a suggestion. What if you continue to work here but you don't take a paycheck? Your earnings would be paid to Unlimited Hidden Treasures?"

I looked at her stunned! How could she suggest something like that? I need my paycheck to live. My mind was racing through what that would look like for me. She saw the surprise on my face and said, "Well, just think about it."

As she turned to walk away, I heard the Lord say to me, "That was not her speaking but Me."

My stunned reaction quickly turned to "God, are you kidding? How will I ever make it?"

That night when I went home from work, I had a chapter of a book, *Leadership 101*, that I had to read before the next day. We had been going through the book as a team at the store. It was to help us to learn and grow as leaders. When I began reading, there was a story in the book about how God had asked a leader to stop taking a paycheck and give their earnings to a charity. He did, and God took care of him financially.

When I read this story, I knew that was God speaking to me, and it was a confirmation that this is what I was to do. This was not a coincidence. It just seemed so incredible to me that God was asking me to do this. But one thing I knew for sure, I could *trust* Him.

When I went to work the next day, first thing in the morning, this lady walked through the front door, and out of her mouth came "Oh, this is a hidden treasure!" The name of our store is Restored Treasures. The name of my nonprofit is Unlimited Hidden Treasures. When she said those words, I knew the Lord was confirming again that I was to partner with Restored Treasures. He was declaring that the two should be one operating side by side.

This meant that I would stop taking a paycheck. My hours would be paid directly to Unlimited Hidden Treasures. It had become so obvious; how could I ignore it? Everything that Megan had said the day before was confirmed.

So that day, I did it. I told Megan I wanted it to start as of June 1. I said to her, "I would rather suffer the consequences of being wrong than to disobey." I really felt at that point that if I didn't do it, I would be disobeying God. And so the journey began with no paycheck.

Chapter 13

FINANCIAL ANSWER COMES

As it began to really settle in what I had done, I began to panic. How will I ever make it? God, will You still provide for me like You have all along?

I knew that God had a strategy for me right where I was at. He had a plan. He would confirm it. I was encouraged once again to wait and listen for what was next.

A few nights later, I had a dream. In the dream, it was very dark outside. I was in my car following a big box truck. I did not have my car lights on even though it was dark. The box truck in front of me was glowing with a light. I was very afraid I couldn't see where I was going or any of the surrounding area because the box truck blocked my view, and the darkness spread out all around me. Somehow I knew as long as my eyes stayed fixed on the back of that truck, it would lead me where I needed to go. I would be safe if I continued to follow that truck. The dream ended.

When I woke up, I knew immediately the interpretation. God was saying to me, "I'm not going to allow you to see ahead and know what is coming." I had to just keep my eyes on him. He was the box truck, and He would lead me. He would keep me safe on this new journey of no paycheck. God is so good to me when He keeps confirming and encouraging me whenever He gives me a new direction that is very scary.

I was given a room at the back of Restored Treasures to set up a production line for making the Operation Christmas Child shoeboxes. We also set up sewing machines to make clothing and bags for each shoebox. I was allowed to pull anything that was donated to the store that could be used for the shoeboxes. Examples of that would be new clothes, material for making clothing or bags, yarn for making hats, and so on.

Setting up the room took time and discipline. I can get excited at first when God has directed me to do something, but then my flesh can get in the way. I tend to get discouraged, overwhelmed, distracted, or just lazy. I have to push myself sometimes to complete a task. Soon it was set up and running.

The night I finished, He woke me up at 5:55 a.m. I knew that He was referring to a scripture verse. I found Isaiah 55:5 (NASB), "Behold, you will call a nation you do not know, a nation which knows you not will run to you, because of the Lord your God, even the Holy One of Israel; for he has glorified you."

What I saw was a call on my life to reach children from another nation that I don't even know!

My first paycheck that went to Unlimited Hidden Treasures was in the amount of $1,555.12. There was that "555" again. The number twelve means divine organization. What an amazing thing He was saying to me. "I have set this up, not you! This is all My doing! You will be reaching children and nations you don't even know."

When that first paycheck for Unlimited Hidden Treasures was placed in my hands, I saw something for the first time. If I had started a resale store on my own, my "profit" at the end of the month would not be as much as I would be getting in these paychecks. Most of my time would have been consumed with operating the store, with much less time and resources available to pour into Unlimited Hidden Treasures. I said, "God you are a genius! Only you." I would never have come up with this solution. My focus is so narrow compared to the wisdom of the Lord. He knows the beginning to the end. He sees the whole picture at one time. We can trust Him completely with everything all the time!

Later, I had another dream about another one of my best friends joining the ministry with us. When I shared the dream with her, she then prayed about it and felt that was what the Lord was showing her to do. So I now have two of my closest friends as partners in the ministry!

The answer came for my finances! By now, the school year was coming to an end, and the two Chinese students that I had would be ending as part of my income. I was also not taking a paycheck at this time. I had no idea what I was going to do next, but I waited on the Lord. There is this scripture, "Nor do we know what to do, but my eyes are on Thee" (2 Chron. 20:12 NASB). I go to that scripture a lot. It brings me peace.

What ended up happening was my parents came to live with me. They are both independent and could take care of themselves, but the home they were living in was not working for their age. They moved into my home. God knew this was coming. I did not. I listened, obeyed, and waited, and He showed up! He is so faithful and can be trusted no matter what!

From the beginning, I knew part of the reason God was sending them was not just for the income but to also work on my character. I knew that it would be challenging, but I knew the Lord would be faithful. What He calls you to do, He will equip you to do.

My parents moved in. After the first night they were there, I was upstairs putting clean sheets on my bed. As I was flinging the top sheet across the bed, I heard the Lord speak, "I am pleased." I knew He was referring to taking my parents. I could have said no, but I don't ever want to say no to God.

When He asks me to do something, even though I know it's going to be hard, it will be so good. He always brings good. I want to obey Him.

The Lord sent a young man from my church the following day. Believe it or not, this was the twin brother to the young man who came earlier in my story with the prophetic word for me. The word was, whatever God calls you to do, He will give the provision to do it.

They look so much alike that I find it very hard to tell them apart. I get it wrong most of the time. He was knocking on my front door. I opened the door and invited him in.

He said to me, "The Lord wants you to know that He loves you very much. He had me buy this gift for you." It was a very large ribbon wick candle. The scent and name of the candle was Amber Fire Light. I love candles! The name of the candle means the presence of God. He just blows me away by the different ways that He shows up and speaks to me, confirming to me again that I was to take my parents in and that His presence would be with me.

There is a recurring theme here that I want to take a moment to expound upon; that is pleasing Him. Each time that I listened and obeyed what He told me to do, it would follow with a message from Him: "I am pleased." It is so important to hear those words from Him. It means we trust Him; therefore, we want to obey Him. It creates that intimate relationship with Him. That's what He wants more than anything. It's what we were created for.

Within a few months of moving in with me, my dad had a heart attack. When I went to the hospital to see him, he was on the third floor. I had never been on the third floor of the hospital before. When I walked into his room, he had a large window with an incredible view. I walked over to the window and saw the view of my entire city! It took my breath away.

The Lord began to speak to me when I looked down below and saw people walking on the sidewalk. They were almost miniature. He said to me, "That is you down there walking, and all you can see is what is in front of you and around you at ground level. This is what I see. This is my view. I can see everywhere with no restriction. So the next time I ask you to do something, and you're afraid because it is an unknown, just trust me. I can see the beginning to the end. You can only see what is right in front of you. You can trust me. I will take care of you."

With experience and a visual like that my trust went deeper.

Chapter 14

NATURAL GAS

My 3,700-square-foot home was heated with a pellet stove and propane furnace. My heating bill was two hundred dollars a month, year round. That bill was draining me.

In the spring, I would buy my wood pellets for my pellet stove because the price is the lowest at that time. I purchased six tons of pellets for my home. That amounts to three hundred forty-pound bags. The bags had to be lifted three times each—once to get them in the car from the store, once to take from the car to inside my home, once to dump inside the hopper. This was an extremely strenuous task to complete alone.

I called up one of my friends and asked him if he would help me. He agreed to do it. When he began picking up the bags, I could see the pain on his face. He had shoulder and knee problems. I felt so bad asking him to help, but I had no one else to turn to. I looked at him and said, "I don't know how or when, but I am believing I will never have to ask you to do this again. I'm believing that this year, I'm done. I'm asking God to make a way for me to not have to do this anymore."

I did not realize until the Lord came and spoke to me about getting rid of the pellet stove that I actually prophesied that day. It was the Lord speaking through me, and it did come to pass. I did get rid of the pellet stove.

In February, I was down in the basement sitting in front of the pellet stove doing my devotions. The Lord began to speak to me and said, "You need to sell the pellet stove. Clear out that room and make it another bedroom to rent out at six hundred dollars a month to add to your income. Then hook up to natural gas."

I thought, *Wow, God, that is genius*. This had never occurred to me.

It would be a more cost-effective way for me to heat the home. Right away, however, I realized that I did not have the funds to make the switch. The last time I checked, it was going to cost five thousand dollars to have natural gas brought to my home. I reminded myself I didn't need to figure that out. I just needed to listen and obey. He had a plan, and who am I to question it.

My old flesh nature wanted to rear up again. I was afraid, and I just didn't want to take the next step. I began doubting and pulling back again. I didn't have the money to do it.

I walk about two miles every morning around my subdivision. When the weather is bad, I walk in the mall. In the morning, there's no one in the mall except walkers.

That morning, I was in the mall. I was going around and was about to pass a garage service door on my right. It's where they take the new cars in and out to display them in the middle of the mall. When my right foot came down and touched the floor, that garage door went up. It startled me so bad. It was an extremely loud noise. I jumped back and looked around. I thought, *What was that?* I'm sure I looked very foolish, but in that moment, the Lord spoke to me. He said, "You must take the next step for the door to open." I could see it as He was talking to me.

So I took the first step toward getting natural gas. I put the pellet stove up for sale. I wanted to wait until I was done using it, but I knew I had to sell it while it was up and running. People want to see it running when they buy an item. I wasn't sure how much I would get out of it because they were not that popular any more. I was shocked when I sold it for half what I had paid for it. Secondly, the gentleman that bought it said I could use it the rest of the season. He wanted it for a cabin down state, and he wouldn't be going there until spring! Only God!

Right from the start, I could see His hand on this project. With the pellet stove out of the room, I began to prepare the room to make it into a bedroom for rent. Next, I called the natural gas company, DTE. I needed to find out what it would cost and when they could do it.

To bring the line up to the house, convert all the appliances, and buy a new hot water heater, the cost would be seven thousand dollars. I can't even tell you where it came from. I just had it, and I was able to pay for it in full. God did it miraculously!

I want to share some of the things that happened along the way. When I called my propane company to tell them that I was switching to natural gas, they were very upset and did not treat me very well. They told me that I would have to pay $125 to pump out whatever gas was left in my tank when I was finished using it.

When I called them to pick up the tank, I knew that I would not get any money back because there was only about 10 percent in the tank. They took their time coming to get the tank after I called them and told them it was ready to be picked up. Within a few weeks after they picked it up, I received a check in the mail from them. I took it out of the envelope and read the receipt to my parents. It read $142 for the gas, $125 charge for pumping it out, and $8.52 for tax. The $125 charge for pumping the remaining out was crossed off, a line right through it. They gave me every single penny for the gas plus the tax.

I said to my parents, "Now that is God!" I have no idea why they did it. There was no explanation, but I know it was God.

Before it was set up for them to come out and run the natural gas line, I realized that I was running very low on propane in the tank. If I had to have them come out and put more in, there's a minimum charge of $250 which I didn't have. Then they would charge me $125 to pump it back out if I didn't use it.

I began praying and crying out to the Lord that I would not run out of propane. The weather at that time was the coldest it had been in a long time. I kept going out and checking the tank almost every day. I tried calling the gas company and asking them to come sooner. They just kept telling me "We will come when we come. You are on the schedule, and we can't move you up any sooner." Part of the issue of their coming was the frost laws were still on.

My dad went out to the tank while I was at work one day, and when I got home, he said to me, "Dianne, you are not going to run out of gas. You're going to be okay. It's going to last until they get here."

I said, "Yeah, okay, Dad. Whatever. I hope you're right."

I left his presence, and I went up to my bedroom. I felt the Lord say to me, "That was Me. I'm your Father, and I'm telling you you're going to be okay."

In the end, I was. I did not run out, and I got every penny back that they said I wouldn't.

As I was waiting for DTE to come out and run the gas line, I kept calling them and asking them to please try and get here sooner. They replied each time, "We can't come any sooner." Within three days after my last call to them, I came home from work, and there were flags up my driveway from MISS DIG. I was so excited when I saw this! I called the gas company and said, "I see MISS DIG has been here. Does that mean you're coming soon?"

She said, "It will be at least two weeks. The next thing to happen is a gentleman will come out and drop white flags right where they're going to put the line. It could be up to two weeks after that before they would get back out and actually put the line in."

I said, "Okay. Thank you." And I hung up.

Three days later, I was getting ready to go to work, and I looked down my driveway. DTE trucks were sitting there. Two men were walking up the driveway.

At that moment, I cried out to the Lord, "Oh, Lord, please let them bypass the white flags. Just let them bypass the white flags. Please, Lord, let them be here today to put the line in."

I went outside and asked the gentleman, "Am I getting gas today, or are you here just to drop the white flags?"

He said, "Ma'am, you're getting gas today!"

I said, "Why aren't you dropping the white flags?"

He replied, "Well, the man who does that is on vacation, and we weren't going to wait for him. We just decided to come get it done."

I looked at him and said, "So you mean you bypassed the white flags?"

He said, "Yes, ma'am!"

I just started cracking up. *God, it's You again!* All along the way, there was favor and blessing from Him to get the gas line in at my house.

Just a few days later, I arrived at work early in the morning. When I turned into the driveway of the store, I was facing east with the sun rising. What I saw in the sky took my breath away. It was a double sun dog in the sky.

A sun dog is a ring that forms around either the sun or the moon, and it has a rainbow look to it. I have seen them before but never a double one. There was a complete ring around the sun, and then when you looked up above the sun, there was another half-moon shape. I got out of my car to take a picture on my phone, and I actually had to walk across the street to capture both of them on the screen.

There were two gentlemen there, and I said to them, "Have you ever seen this?"

They said, "No, we haven't." They were just as amazed as I was. It was so beautiful.

I shared earlier in my story that God continues to tell and show me that I will have a double portion of blessings in my life. I knew that because I had stepped out in faith to start the natural gas line coming to my home that He was showing me again you're going to receive a double blessing. Throughout the natural gas hookup, I would see double blessings. God was faithful through to the end of the project. Even when it seems impossible, He makes it possible.

Chapter 15

TIME FOR ANOTHER MOVE

As soon as that project was done, the Lord began to speak to me about what He wanted to do next. He is always speaking and moving. It is a matter of, are we listening? If we aren't, we will miss our next assignment from Him. Sometimes it's hard to keep up. I tell my friends all the time, "With God, I have learned to strap on my seat belt and hang on!"

He spoke to me one morning while reading my devotions. The devotion was based on the scripture 2 Timothy 4:5 (NASB), "But you, be sober in all things, endure hardship, do the work of an evangelist, fulfill your ministry." As I read the last words, "fulfill your ministry," I knew that the Lord was speaking to me. I knew it was about the ministry He had called me to, Operation Christmas Child. I took a moment to talk to the Lord, and I said to Him, "Lord, I have done all I can do."

We were currently operating out of the room that I was given at Restored Treasures. We had grown out of it, and we needed to move. Our next move would be into the pole barn which is on my property. In order for us to operate year round in the pole barn, we would have to insulate first and get a heater.

Remember I had a renter in my pole barn using it for storage. He was now paying me $350 a month. I needed that income along with the income I was getting from my parents and my two ladies in the basement for my daily living expenses.

I continued my conversation with the Lord, saying, "There is electricity in the pole barn, and I got the natural gas to the pole barn when I brought it up to the house. The next thing is, my renter would have to move out. I will do that when You give me the same income coming from somewhere else. You have to replace it because I can't live without that income." I felt I had to explain to Him why I couldn't tell my renter to leave, as if He needed that. I knew in my heart what He wanted me to do. I just thought how could He be taking away more income when the opposite should be happening. Once again, I would have to trust Him. But I was really struggling to actually do that.

Well, over the course of the next three days, no matter what I said, did, or saw, it was all saying the same thing—"Move forward," meaning have your renter leave the pole barn. I argued with God because I needed that income.

It was so scary! A big step! I called my friend and told her what I felt the Lord was saying to me. I said, "I don't want to do it. I'm scared. It doesn't make sense. Would you please pray about it and see if the Lord gives you anything?"

A few hours later that same day, she called me. She said, "I was praying about what you had shared with me this morning, and when I had a moment at work, I offered it up to the Lord. I immediately had a vision. I saw you jumping out of an airplane. The parachute deployed. You were very gently gliding down to the ground. You had joy and peace on your face. You had no fear."

I knew what it meant. I knew I was to take a giant leap of faith, and the Lord would be there to gently guide me and give me peace. That leap of faith was to get my renter out of my pole barn so we could move Unlimited Hidden Treasures in. How could I say no to that when it seemed so obvious where it came from and what I was to do.

I said to my friend, "How in the world is He going to do this? It's going to be *big*." I had not a penny to put toward it, and there was no money in the nonprofit account to cover any of it. So He would have to do it all. I knew it would be about $12,000 to do what needed to be done.

I called my renter that very day and told him I would need him to move out as I needed the building for operating my ministry. I thought he might be upset or try to argue with me, but instead, he did the opposite. He said, "Absolutely. I'm on vacation right now, but when I get back home, I will start right away looking for a place to go."

When I got off the phone, I had mixed emotions. I was very excited about this new step and direction but, at the same time, very concerned. I had two questions: how will the pole barn get done, and how will I make it financially?

When I shared this next big step of faith with my manager at work, she looked at me and said, "Why are you doing this? Why do you not take a paycheck and live on almost nothing?"

I have found that when a question is posed like that, it's not the person themselves asking it; it's God. He already knows the answer. It's for you. What it does is make you answer out loud. That way, you are saying it and hearing it. It's for your benefit. It gets it deep inside your heart. It's not just coming from your head but your heart as well.

My answer back to her was "How can I not? Do you know the story and my testimony?"

She said, "No."

So I shared it with her. God placed a call on my life fifteen years back. I heard His voice speak to me, "This is your ministry." I shared everything with her that I wrote in the Operation Christmas Child chapter.

From the moment I said yes to the call, I began to experience one miracle after another. My life was so radically changed. So I said to her, "How can I not do this? This is a true call of God on my life. There is a drive inside of me to do it. I can't do anything else. I also feel I have the anointing from Him to do it." The question that was asked and the conversation that took place after was for me. It was to solidify the calling on my life inside of me.

I want to take a moment to share more about the anointing. Within a few weeks after I had packed the first ten shoeboxes and heard God say "This is your ministry," I received an anointing.

Two close friends of mine were going to take a trip to Pensacola, Florida, to go to the Brownsville revival that was going on. They asked me to go along. I didn't want to go because I had all four boys at the time, and they were all still young. I didn't want to leave them.

The husband of one of my friends that asked me to go said, "Well, are you going to go?"

I said, "No."

He said, "Did you pray about it?"

I had to say no because I hadn't. I felt convicted, and I said, "Okay, I will pray about it."

The next morning as I was headed to kneel at the couch for prayer, I heard the Lord speak. He said, "You must go to Brownsville to receive an anointing." I didn't even know what an anointing was, but I knew I heard His voice, and I was to go. So I went.

The first night we were there, when the service was all over, my friends stood up to leave. All of a sudden, out of nowhere, across the back of my shoulders, there was a very hot heat. I told them what was happening, and they said my face was very red.

I said, "I don't feel anything on my face, only my shoulders."

One of my friends said, "Heat represents anointing."

When she said that, I remembered hearing the Lord say to me, "You must go to Brownsville to receive an anointing." It lasted for a few minutes, and then it was gone. I just pondered what had happened. We then left and went back to the motel for the night.

That night, I had a dream. In the dream, I was a bride. I was in a wedding dress waiting for a limo to come pick me up. The limo pulled up, and the driver got out, came to the house, and opened the front door. He took me out to the limo and put me in the front passenger seat. He got in and shut the door. I turned around and looked in the back seat. As far as I could see, there were rows and rows of people. It was like the car had no end. There were men and women alike. They were all looking at me and smiling. The dream ended.

The interpretation of the dream is this. The bride is the church, God's people. The limo held the endless number of people who would be fed by the church. The driver is the Lord. He came and took me to join Him in a ministry that would affect all the people that I turned around and had seen in the back of the limo.

It was then that I connected the two. The anointing was for the ministry that He had called me to—Operation Christmas Child. All the people in the dream are those that will receive shoeboxes and be impacted by it. So here in the very beginning, God showed me what the end result would be if I said yes to what He was calling me to.

Within seven days of calling my renter and asking him to move out of the pole barn, I got word that my parents were going to be moving out and moving back into their own home in Central Lake.

My older brother had come down and shared with my parents that he wanted to retire. He needed a part-time job. He wanted to know if they wanted to go back into their home, and he would take care of them as a part-time job. They were elated and said yes! It would take a few months before they could move back into their home as there was some work that would have to be done on the home.

For me, this was very hard to hear and receive. This was more of my monthly income being lost. First, the income from the pole barn, and now from my parents as well. *God, what are You doing?* This should be going the opposite way. Gaining more, not losing more? How would I make it? Here I am again!

Two nights later, I had a dream that was very interesting. In the dream, my home was lifted up off of the ground. It was whirling around in the air and was thrown out onto a lake that was next to it.

The interpretation of the dream was that God was changing the direction and purpose of my home. That didn't come as a surprise to me because He would have to do something major with all of my income being taken away. All I had left for income would be the two ladies in the basement. I asked God, "What are You doing? What are You saying? Because I just want to join You. It's not about me. It's always about You!"

Before I left to go to work the next morning, I stopped down at the pole barn to take another look. I walked inside, took some measurements, and then ran some calculations. Just as I had guessed, this would most likely cost $12,000. I was instantly afraid and discouraged. How could this ever happen? I got in my car and went to work. Before I got out of my car to go in, I just sat there a minute. I felt everything crashing in on me. I said, "Lord, how is this possible? How will this ever happen? How am I going to make it?" I began to cry. Just then, my phone beeped with an email from my best friend, Anna. I opened it to find she had sent me her devotion from that morning. It was titled "A Dream Come True." It said,

> God has an idea. Determines His will. Then brings it to pass in teaching us to move after the pattern of His workings. He begins by giving us His idea. We receive it as a dream. His Holy Spirit impresses us with a certainty that this idea is His will. As soon as an idea from God is known to be the will of God, His word tells us exactly what to do. Pray your will be done on earth as it is in heaven. From that time on, what you know He sees as an already accomplished fact begins more and more to appear to you in the same condition. DONE! A dream come true! Praise follows on the heels of prayer. Dream on.

I was so lifted at that moment. Fear was gone! I was filled with great hope and faith because I knew it wasn't my friend who had sent me the devotion; it was God Himself. He was confirming and reassuring me that I was to keep moving forward in what He was telling me to do. It was His will for me. He would complete the pole barn and take care of all my needs financially. It was "DONE!"

The next morning, I found out that my parents would most likely be moving even sooner than originally thought. Again my first instinct was to give in to the fear. How do I figure this out? How do I make this work?

When I went to bed that night, I spoke out loud and said, "I refuse to be afraid, and I refuse to figure it out. Lord, it is all yours, and I trust you." Fear was gone, and I went right to sleep.

The very next morning as I was taking my walk before going into work, a friend called me. She said to me, "God has spoken to me in prayer this morning. There were three things He told me to do."

I said, "Okay, tell me."

She said, "The first thing is I am waiving your house payments to me until the first of next year. Second, I have $2,200 in cash I want to give you to help pay for your immediate bills. Third, I want to give $1,000 a month until the end of the year for Unlimited Hidden Treasures."

I was so taken aback that I began to cry. I said, "Thank you. I am so shocked because you have no idea that just last night, I found out more of my income was going to be taken away. You didn't know I had spoken to the Lord that I refused to be afraid, and I refused to figure it out. I just gave it to Him. I'm just in awe how He has answered my cries so quickly."

Those two phrases, "I refuse to be afraid" and "I refuse to figure it out," have been my go-to ever since. When I apply them, there is peace and joy. I can relax. When I don't choose those two things, I am in fear and turmoil. My brain is constantly trying to figure it out. I have learned to completely surrender everything to Him. He can have it, and He can figure it out.

My parents had not moved out yet and were still in my home with me. My father said to me one morning, "What are you going to do when we move out? You're no longer getting the income from the pole barn. You won't get income from us, and you don't take a paycheck at work. How are you going to make it?"

I said, "Dad, I don't know, but God knows, and He has a plan."

With my father's words on my mind, I left the house and got into my car to leave for work. I turned the radio on and immediately heard these words in a song:

> *My life is built on your faithfulness.*
> *My hope is held in your promises.*
> *I take each step with your confidence cuz I am yours.*
> *I am yours.*
> *You never fail. You never will.*

I trust your name for greater things.
You will come through. You always do.
You clear the way in the wilderness.
You brought me back from my brokenness.
You took my shame and buried it.
What you've done I won't forget.
I will not fear for you are with me.
I've seen this fight from the victory.
No power of hell can stand against me…

I was laughing and crying so hard going down the road as these words were being played in my ear. I just kept repeating "God, only You, only You could do this. Only You would speak to me this way with just such power and assurance again." The song is "Greater Things" by Mack Brock.

So at this time, I am waiting on the Lord for the finances for the pole barn and for my personal income. It is not easy waiting. But He is always faithful.

My renter was in the process of moving out of the pole barn. I came home from work one day, and when I passed the pole barn on my way up to the house, I looked over and saw that the door had been left open, and the light was on. I waited for the rest of the day, hoping he would come back and shut the door and turn the light off, but he never did. So I walked down to the pole barn to shut the light off and shut the door. As I was doing that, the Lord spoke to me.

He said, "I have opened that door, and I am directing you to move in." I tell you there is something about doors! God uses them a lot to speak to me. I love it! The light being left on represented Him and that He had left the door open. He was speaking and directing me to move in even when I didn't want to.

The reason I didn't want to move in was because it was not finished yet. It had to be insulated and the furnace hooked up. I wanted to wait until these things were done because I didn't want to have to move everything in and turn around and move it all back out so this work could be done. There would be truckloads of stuff that we would be moving in. It just made a lot more sense to me to wait.

But what I've learned from the Lord in the past is, it doesn't have to make sense when you're working with Him. You can't use human reasoning and logic. He just doesn't operate that way.

It makes me think of the scripture in Isaiah 55:8–9 (NASB), "'For My thoughts are not your thoughts, neither are your ways My ways,' declares the Lord. 'For as the heavens are higher than the earth, so are My ways higher than your ways, and My thoughts than your thoughts.'"

So the moment my renter moved out, we moved Unlimited Hidden Treasures in. I felt there was an urgency to do that. The move was complete. Now the mandate was to wait and listen for His voice of what to do next.

Chapter 16

COMPLETED IN 52 DAYS

We were moved in and were back in operation in just a few days. At the time of the move, we had just completed all the boxes we had made for that year and delivered them to the collection center in town. Now we could begin on next year's boxes.

Our inventory of handmade bags and dresses was depleted. So we were going to take the next two months and just sew. By Jan 1, we would have to start packing again in order to get them all done by November of next year.

The weather turned really cold very early that year. Without heat in the building, we had to do something else. I said, "Lord, what am I to do now?" He showed me the solution was to move up to my house and set the sewing machines up at my kitchen table for now. I thought, *Oh yeah, we can do that.* It made sense because all we were doing was sewing and not packing. So that was what we did.

After several weeks of this, we got an early snowstorm, and some of the ladies could not drive up my driveway because it's so steep and slippery. I said, "Lord, what am I going to do now?" He showed me to go to Pam's home. She is one of the friends He called to partner with me. She only lives two miles from my house. I said, "Okay." Her home would only work for us until the first of January. After that, she would be leaving for Arizona for the remainder of the winter.

I was feeling a sense from the Lord to join in agreement in prayer with the ladies about our next move. I felt Him show me to pray, asking and believing Him to prepare the pole barn before my friend had to leave. We were to pray we would not be going back to my house but into the pole barn to work throughout the winter. I knew that was a big bold prayer that seemed impossible. But nothing is impossible for Him. So we all joined in agreement in prayer. That was on Friday.

I had gotten one quote to insulate the pole barn, and it was $14,000. We really needed the spray foam, not the fiberglass insulation. We also needed a furnace and the cost of hooking it up. There was no money in the nonprofit account for that, and obviously, I had no money myself. The next day, Saturday, I got a call from a gentleman I had called earlier to obtain a second quote. We agreed to meet later that afternoon.

I was in Pam's car when I took the call. We were on our way to Dollar General to purchase a treasure of items at a great discount for the shoeboxes. When I hung up from arranging the quote, I asked Pam to pray with me. I asked the Lord that when the contractor came, he would not see me, he would not see the ministry of Operation Christmas Child or the pole barn. I asked the Lord that he would see Him and what He was doing. I prayed the Lord would show this contractor how He wanted him to join Him. I asked the Lord to reveal Himself to this gentleman.

When he arrived, we were in the process of unloading and packing the abundance of items we had purchased. I showed him around the pole barn and told him what we were doing. We could tell by the questions he was asking and the way he was looking at us that he was encountering the Lord like we had prayed.

He said to me, "I will have a quote for you by Monday." When he left, we all were very excited because we truly felt he was going to be the one that God would call to do this job.

When we finished putting away the clothes we had just purchased from Dollar General, I went back up to the house. The other two ladies went home. I went into the living room and sat down on the couch.

The moment I did, the Lord spoke to me. I heard "Fifty-two days." When I heard that, I immediately remembered back in January of that year the Lord had spoken those words to me. He told me fifty-two days, and the pole barn would be done once it was started. He used the story of Nehemiah to speak this to me. When Nehemiah built the wall, it was done in fifty-two days. It was something that was impossible to do, but God did it. So I wrote this down in my journal and pondered it in my heart.

Now sitting on the couch, hearing that word again, I said, "No, God, that can't be! Are you saying to me in fifty-two days the pole barn will be done?" I brought the calendar up on my phone and counted the days. The date was November 9. There were twenty-one days left in November. The month of December has thirty-one days. Together they total fifty-two days.

Remember my friend would be leaving January 1. The prayer just the day before was that we would leave January 1 and go right into the pole barn from there. I just was in awe, and I felt the Lord was confirming that this would be the man to do the job, even though he had not even given us the quote yet, even though we did not have one penny to go toward it.

So Monday came, and I was very excited to hear the quote. But when he called, he said, "I want to meet in person with you to give you the quote. So when is your next day off from work?"

I said, "Thursday." I was disappointed I would have to wait until Thursday.

Thursday finally came, and we met down in the pole barn. He started the conversation by saying, "Well, the bad news is that it's going to cost ten thousand dollars. The good news is I'm covering it."

When he said that, it was almost like someone had hit me in the gut. I doubled over and stepped back. I began to cry. I said to him, "Are you saying to me you are going to do this for free?"

He said, "Yes." I did not know what to say. It was overwhelming.

I said to him, "Did the Lord speak to you?"

He said, "Oh yeah."

I said, "What did He say?"

He said, "When I left that day from the pole barn after looking it over, I got out to my truck to leave, and the Lord spoke to me. He said, 'You are to help these ladies.'" He then began to weep. "Just give me a minute." And he turned away. I think he was ashamed that he was crying.

I said to him, "Please, no, don't. You are an amazing man. You are allowing the Holy Spirit to come on you like this." We both stood there in awe because we were in the presence of God and what He was doing. No words can describe it.

He said, "Push everything to one side, and I will be back not this Saturday but the next to get that half done. Once we have that half done, you can move the things over to the other side. We will then come back and finish the other side."

I was shocked. The work could be done with all that we had inside. Remember how I didn't want to move in because I was sure we'd have to move everything out so the building could be insulated. I fought God on moving in. Well, once again, He knew more than me and knew we would not have to do that. Sometimes I get so upset with myself questioning God when I should never do that. Just listen and obey.

I texted him on the following Monday to tell him that we had pushed everything to one side, and we were ready for him to insulate that half. He texted me right back. He said, "I have had an accident on the job, and I am in the hospital."

I knew immediately what was going on. Oh my goodness, the enemy had poured out his wrath on this poor man for partnering with God to do this for us.

I have experienced this over and over and over again in my life. The moment I say yes to God doing what He has told me to do, I am a target for the enemy. But I do not allow it to stop me. I keep moving forward with more tenacity than ever. If the enemy is fighting me that hard, it's got to be something good that I'm doing for Him. The next chapter is devoted to speaking on just this.

I texted him right back and said, "I am so sorry. I know who this is, and I'm going to get my prayer warriors praying for you right away." I figured that this would really put the work off, and it would not be done for quite some time. But once again, I was shocked.

He returned a text right back saying, "The work is going to go on. My son will be there on Saturday." His son came, and it got done. We moved everything to the other half, and his son came back and finished the other half. We were all just in awe of what God had done. The absolute impossible became possible with God.

The following Sunday, I went to church and was handed a one-thousand-dollar check for the furnace. Once again, I found myself just in shock. I did not know at the time that I got the check for the furnace, someone else had already bought a brand-new furnace and was waiting for the insulation to get done to bring it to me. There was that double portion again.

He is so awesome! He is so amazing! Something so huge, and God showed up and did it like it was nothing. We were in the pole building in *fifty-two* days! God did it just like He had built the wall for Nehemiah. Utterly, totally, completely impossible, but He did it. We anticipate being able to pack and ship more shoeboxes than we had ever been able to before.

Chapter 17

WE ARE A TARGET OF THE ENEMY WHEN WE ARE IN GOD'S WILL

The gentleman who insulated the pole barn was a target of the enemy's wrath. He had agreed to step into the will of God by insulating the pole building and getting it ready for us to start packing boxes. He was severely hurt and laid up for a long time all because he heard the voice of God and obeyed.

I have seen and experienced this over and over again in my life. If you have fully surrendered your life to the Lord, and you are walking out the call on your life, then you are a target for the enemy.

We do not have to be afraid of this. We do not have to figure out what we're going to do because God's got it. The enemy knows he has to go through God to get to us. So nothing comes to us that doesn't pass through our Father's hands first. God is on our side.

My journey with being in the wrath of the enemy starts at my birth. I was a placenta previa baby. Back then, it was very common for the baby and mother to die from this. The doctor told my mom we would just have to wait and see if I would make it or not. I would have to push past the placenta. There just wasn't much more they could do. I did make it through by the hand of God.

The enemy knew the call I had on my life. He knew the advancement of the kingdom the Operation Christmas Child shoeboxes would have. So from birth, the enemy sought to take me out, and that was the first attempt that failed.

When I was about seven years old, my mom gave me a round hard piece of peppermint candy. She also gave one to my brother. We went into the living room, and we were laughing and jumping on the furniture. My candy got stuck in my throat. I could not talk. I could not get air. So I walked out into the kitchen where my mom was and pointed at my mouth. She knew right away what had happened.

Back then, we didn't have the Heimlich maneuver. So she bent me over and just started pounding my back. It would not dislodge. By this time, I was turning blue and ready to pass out. So my mom took her hand and shoved it down my throat as far as she could. She said she just felt the tip of the candy. By her touching it, that was enough to move and dislodge it. I was okay.

The third attempt to take me out was just shortly after we moved to Traverse City. It started with a dream that the Lord gave me three nights before it actually happened. In the dream was myself and my sister. We each had a time card in our hands. She went first and handed her time card to the Lord. He took her card. I came up behind her and handed my card to Him. He gave it right back to me. I was very happy about it. The same thing happened three times in the dream. The dream ended. When I woke up, I said, "Lord, what are You saying to me?"

I heard "I'm redeeming the time."

I had to look up the word *redeeming*. It has two meanings, to buy back or to make the most of. I truly felt that I was making the most of my time, so I didn't feel it could be that. But to buy back? It didn't make sense? I didn't understand? I had the dream on a Friday night, so I pondered it all weekend. I didn't know what the Lord was saying to me until it happened on Monday.

It was a winter day, and the snow was coming down thick and slushy. The roads were very slippery. I took my kids to school and dropped them off. I then proceeded to go to the grocery store. When I was done at the store, I headed back home. There is a ninety-degree corner in the road I had to go through to get home. As I started into the corner going very slowly, a truck coming the opposite direction was going way too fast to make the corner. I could tell we were going to hit head on. There was nothing I could do to get out of the way. When I knew we were going to hit, I closed my eyes. I didn't want to see it. I was waiting for the crash but didn't hear anything. I thought maybe God miraculously took them out of the way! Then we hit! The next thing I knew, I was pushed back and lifted up in my seat. I was now viewing the crash looking down from the ceiling of the van. I was not taken out of the van, but I was at the top looking down. I saw both airbags deploy. Within seconds, I was sitting back down in the seat. I then looked up and watched as the roof of the van began to crinkle up under the impact. The impact was so powerful I could actually feel my brain sloshing around in my head.

Once everything stopped, I tried to get out of the van. The doors were jammed all the way around. I had to wait for a fireman to come and break the window to get me out. The only injury that I had was when I was put back down in my seat. My right knee hit the dashboard and swelled up. I was wearing my seat belt.

When the police got there, an officer took me to his patrol car and set me in the front seat to write out the accident report.

My husband at the time was called to the scene. When he got there, he squatted down next to me where I was sitting in the front seat. The police officer looked over at him and said, "Your bride is the innocent victim here today." I knew the minute he said that it was the voice of God speaking through him to me. I recognized my Father's voice.

From the moment I was hit, questions were repeating over and over in my mind. What have I done? What did I do wrong that this happened? Have I offended God in some way? Was He mad at me? Why did God allow this?

When the police officer gave the answer that he did, it shut those questions down. It also triggered my memory of the dream. The Lord was saying directly to me through the police officer that I was the innocent victim there today.

I now understood the dream. In the dream, the enemy was trying to take my life, but each time I handed my time card in, it was given back to me. My Father was saying, "No, Satan, she is mine.

You can't take her!" I know and believe the enemy can never take your life without getting permission from the Lord. We do not have to ever be afraid or worried because God is on our side. He will protect and defend us. Isaiah 43:1 (NASB) says, "Do not fear, for I have redeemed you; I have called you by name; you are mine!"

The van I was driving was totaled. My husband said, "I just can't believe you don't have any seat belt or airbag damage to your body."

I said, "That's because I wasn't in my seat belt when the impact came. The Lord had pushed me back and up away from the seat belt and airbag." He truly saved and protected me that day from the enemy!

I have so many more stories of attack, but I will finish with this last one.

We have a local minor baseball team called The Beach Bums. They partnered with Operation Christmas Child one night as a fundraiser for the ministry. They asked me to throw out the first pitch. I was managing a campground that was an hour away at that time. I drove to the event that night, and it was a great success! I am not even going to write about the first pitch. That was actually a big embarrassment. We all had a good time, and over $1,500 was raised for the ministry. It was as I was driving home that the attack came.

As I was heading out of town back to the campground, I was traveling on a double-lane road. A car came flying up behind me, and I was in the left lane at the time. He tried ramming my car several times. I was watching from my rearview mirror. I could not get over because I had a car right beside me. He continued to try to ram my car, so I had to speed up to get into the right lane and let him pass. I had no idea what his problem was.

We were halfway back now and traveling on a single-lane road with dense trees on both sides. Out of nowhere, in one bound, a deer came out and was about to leap again which would put him right smack in front of my car to hit. I screamed, "Jesus!" I closed my eyes because I didn't want to see it.

When there was no collision, I opened my eyes, and the deer was gone! My son who was in the front passenger's seat next to me said, "Mom, why didn't that deer hit us? Why, Mom?"

I said, "I only know that at the name of Jesus, everything must bow the knee. God must have miraculously taken him out of our path." That deer should have hit us right in the middle of the car. There is no other explanation but *God*!

We had only gone another five miles down the road when we encountered a motorcycle accident. There are two ninety-degree corners in this stretch of road. As we came out of the first corner and looked ahead to the next corner, I saw a motorcycle lying on its side and a body close to it. When I pulled up and got out of the car, I ran to the woman who was lying next to the motorcycle. I bent down and literally watched her take her last breath. The man driving the motorcycle was lying in the ditch a long way from the bike. He was drunk.

Had we only been a few minutes earlier on that road, we would have been in that accident, and I shudder to think what the outcome would have been. I thought of the two encounters we had before this one. I felt because of them, it kept us from being part of this accident.

When I got back into the car, my son said to me, "Mom, what is happening? Why has all of this stuff happened to us? Can we please just get back to the campground?"

Just like my son, I was very shaken by the whole evening and what had taken place. I knew the enemy wanted to take us out, but God was our shield. He is our protector and defender!

The last thing I want to share sums it all up.

My friend Anna was diagnosed twice with cancer. Both times, she went through treatment and is cancer free today. She is what I would call an evangelist. Wherever she goes, her antenna is up for an opportunity to share the gospel message and lead them to salvation.

We were in church one Sunday, and an altar call had just been given at the end of the service. My friend Anna was called upon to step up beside this person who had come up to receive prayer for salvation. She would pray with and lead them to the Lord. As she stepped out of her pew and headed toward the front, the Lord spoke to me.

I was standing right behind where she was sitting. I heard the Lord say, "Not even a cancer diagnosis can keep her from fulfilling the call I have on her life."

There is nothing and no one who can stop you from fulfilling what God has called you to do. You are the only one who can stop the call. The only way you can stop it is through disobedience. I don't care what the enemy fires at you; it can't stop you. Just keep your eyes on Him and do what He is telling you to do no matter the cost.

Chapter 18

DIVINE APPOINTMENT AND DREAM

In the midst of waiting for God to show up and give me more income, I had an idea. I thought if He didn't show up by the time my finances ran out, I would sell the house. Well, the Lord quickly took selling the house off the table.

I had been selling some items on Marketplace for Operation Christmas Child. I had a lady who wanted to purchase some dishes that I had posted. So she came over to pick them up. She came up my driveway and parked just outside my house. I saw her coming, so I went outside to meet her at her vehicle. The things that she came to buy were down from the house in a shed by the pole barn.

As I was walking toward her, she was getting out of her car. I said, "Ma'am, we're going to be going down to that shed to get the things that you purchased."

As she got out of the car, she said out loud, "Oh my word, your view is amazing." My house sits way up on a hill. I have a view of two bays and the city below. It really is stunning. As she handed me the money for the items she purchased, she put her business card on top. So when I took the money, I saw the card. She is a realtor. She said to me, "Would you ever consider selling?"

My head was saying, *Yes, there's my financial rescue.* But my heart was going in the opposite direction because the Lord told me not to sell. I said, "No, I'm not selling."

She said, "I have a buyer I am working with right now that would love this!"

I said again, "No, I am not selling." I was curious as to the value of my home, so I said, "Would you just like to come and see it."

She said, "Yes, can I?"

We came into the house, and I showed her the living room, dining room, and kitchen area first. We then started down the hall to the bedrooms. She stopped halfway down the hall, turned to me, and said, "I feel the anointing. This house is anointed. This is God's house. You can't sell it."

I said to her, "Are you a believer?"

She said, "Absolutely!" She then said, "When I got out of the car, I felt like I stepped into His presence." I was shocked! I had never met this woman before. It was very powerful what she was saying about the house.

We continued through the house. At one point, she shared what she felt the house was worth. The figure that she gave me meant I would have about five hundred thousand dollars equity in my home.

We then went outside and down to the shed to get the items that she had purchased. She was looking up at the house from the shed and said one more time, "This is God's house, and you can't sell it." She gathered her purchases and left.

When she left, I said to the Lord, "This was You. What are You saying to me? Am I to sell or keep the house?"

He spoke to me and said, "This was a huge temptation for you to sell the house because it would answer all your financial issues. It was a huge temptation for her because she could sell the house in a day and reap the profit. That is why I had to manifest myself in such a strong way through her. It was me speaking through her to make it very clear to both of you. I own this house, and you are not to sell it."

"Okay, Lord, that is off the table, and I will not consider it again." I then said to the Lord, "Okay, if I can't sell the house, then what are You going to do to meet my financial situation? Lord, I need You to show up soon!" Within a very short time, He gave me three dreams in one night.

In the dream, I was standing just outside the front entrance of the home that I grew up in. This home was built very close to the main road. Where I was looking, I saw a big ball of bright light. In the midst of that light, I saw a plane tire fall down out of the sky and land right in front of me. This tire reminded me of a Cessna tire. It was very small with a half-moon shaped metal over it. When it hit the ground, it rolled to my right off in the distance into a lake. In real life, that lake was where my father would always plant our garden. Now in the dream, it is a very deep lake. The tire disappeared in the water. That was the end of the first dream.

The second dream was exactly the same, only the tire that fell from the sky was now bigger. It reminded me of a passenger plane tire, so just a little bigger than the first one. It hit the ground and did the same thing, rolled off to my right into the lake. That was the end of the dream.

The third dream was exactly the same. This time, however, there were two tires. This reminded me of a Boeing 747 tire. When it hit the ground, it rolled off to my right and disappeared in the lake. This time as I watched the tire roll into the lake, I noticed the first tire that fell from the sky was now floating in the lake. That was the end of the dream.

When I woke up, I had no idea what these three dreams meant. So I called my pastor friend who has the gift of interpreting dreams.

The first three dreams took place at the home that I grew up in. That means it's about me. The tires represent it's on the move. So it is happening now. The tires represent gifts that God is going to give to me. The reason the first one was floating was because He has already given it to me. I knew right away what that was. That one represented the gift of getting my home and pole barn hooked up to natural gas. Each of the tires got bigger as they came, which represents the gifts would increase as they come.

The garden represents food to feed me. It's now a lake, which represents the Holy Spirit. So the Holy Spirit is feeding me. I knew in the dream that the lake was very deep, even though I couldn't see the depth, and no one told me. The depth is unfathomable because it's the Holy Spirit. The depth of the Holy Spirit is unfathomable.

I was so excited about this dream! What is coming next? What is the second tire? At the time that I had the dream, the pole barn had not been completed yet. So that was the second tire. The cost of the natural gas line was about $7,000, and the pole barn was about $12,000.

Now I was waiting for the third tire to be revealed. What would it be?

While I was waiting for the revealing of the third tire, I had another dream. This dream was the night before the pandemic COVID-19 lockdown. The very next morning after the dream was the last day I would work. My store was shut down for exactly two months.

In the dream, Pam, my ministry partner, was standing there with a sign in her hand. The sign read, "My Dream 88." She then spoke to me and said, "The president says this to you for this year." That was the end of the dream.

The number eight means eternity (Him), new beginnings, super abundant, even satiating. The word *satiating* means to satisfy a need, a desire, fully or to excess. Two eights means double portion. I wasn't sure what was meant by "My Dream" or the president saying this to me for this year. But I knew it would be revealed when it was time for me to know. I knew this had something to do with the plane tire dream, but I just couldn't put it all together.

So while I was waiting for that revelation, I was experiencing something else at the same time. Something amazing began to unfold that led to and confirmed both the "third tire" dream and the "88" dream. They were both connected.

I called my prayer warrior friend Sarah. I told her my financial situation, and as we went into prayer, she said, "Lord, Dianna needs a windfall. Let it fall right out of the sky."

I interrupted her and said, "What is a windfall?"

She said, "Well, it's like receiving a large amount of money coming out of nowhere."

I honestly had never heard of that term before, but when she described what it meant, I thought of my dream of the tires. They just fell out of the sky! I knew my friend had just prophesied in her prayer.

In the meantime, I had several friends that kept telling me to apply for unemployment while I was off work because of the virus. I did not think I would be eligible, nor was it right for me to apply. So I fought doing it. Then one day, I felt prompted by the Lord to apply.

I asked my friend Pam, the same one who had stood in my dream holding the sign, if she would help me fill out the application online. At this point, I had been out of work for over ten weeks. The answer came back immediately that I qualified, and I would be getting all ten weeks at once. The total was $4,880! She turned to me and said, "There is your windfall!"

The moment she said that, my mind went immediately to both dreams. Oh my goodness, there is the meaning and revelation of both dreams. The "My Dream 88" sign was referring to the third tire dream. Remember double tires (88). It was the "My Dream" that I had. It was my friend holding the sign who helped me sign up for unemployment. All the money "windfall" came from the president. It was also no coincidence the unemployment amount was *$4,880*—"88." So there was my third tire, financial answer, and my windfall.

I didn't just get the unemployment; I also got the stimulus check of $1,200! In total from both the stimulus check and unemployment, it was $7,600! Who could ever even imagine that out of a pandemic, I would receive $7,600.

Shortly after this was over, I was reading 1 Kings 17:6 (NASB), "And the ravens brought him bread and meat in the morning and bread and meat in the evening, and he drank from the brook." This was during a worldwide drought. I said, "Lord, just as you fed Elijah during a worldwide drought, you will supply my needs during a worldwide pandemic!" Amazing!

This financial provision was wonderful! It got me through until God sent me an aviation college student. With his monthly income, I could at least meet my monthly bills, but nothing above that.

I did not realize until the following winter after I took out my pellet stove there was a problem. I did not realize how much the pellet stove heated my home. With that gone and a very cold winter, the furnace that I had was not enough to keep the house warm. It could only bring the house up to 68 on the main floor which left it at 63 in the basement for my lady renters. This was not acceptable. The only solution was a new furnace. Oh boy, here I go again.

The Lord repeatedly told me to move forward and get a new furnace. I got a quote. and it was going to be $8,500. I had to have a 120,000-btu furnace to heat my 3,700-square-foot home. Wow! How can I do it? I only had $4,500 from unemployment. I was told I could get a loan interest free for one year if I made the same payment every month for that year. If I didn't make that monthly payment, the interest would kick in at a very high rate.

I went ahead and figured out what my payment would be a month if I did it. I fell over when I saw that amount. It would be $333.33333333333333! Even though I could not make that payment, the 333 is the Father, Son, and Holy Spirit repeating for infinity. How could I deny that? I paid the down payment to get me scheduled on the calendar as the heating and cooling business was months out on their work.

By the time the two months came, and the furnace was installed, two people stepped in and paid the remaining balance in full! I never even had to make the first payment!

I called the couple that paid the bulk of the balance. I said, "You don't have that kind of money. How can you do this?"

They both laughed and said, "We know that, but God told us to do it. We can't wait to see what He is going to do next. We feel so blessed to be part of what He is doing!" Wow, talk about being humble! I am so thankful when those around me are obedient to the voice of God when He speaks to them.

I never need to fear or try to figure out the provision that I need for living my daily life. God is sufficient for all my needs. He has proven that to me over and over again as you have read. So when this provision runs out, He will supply for my next needs.

So the journey and the adventure continues, and I cannot wait to see what He will provide for me next!

Chapter 19

THE PROMISE

At this point in my life, I have been divorced for seven years. The number seven means complete. So I felt that this year, I would receive the promise that the Lord gave me seven years ago. That promise was a godly husband.

I love the story in the Bible that is found in the book of Ruth. It is a wonderful love story that only God could orchestrate. You enter into a story where both husbands have died, Ruth's and Naomi's (her mother-in-law). Naomi made a decision to go back to her home country because there was nothing left for her where she was at. Ruth made the decision to follow Naomi. Ruth chose to leave behind her home, culture, and religion to take up her mother-in-law's faith and home. Ruth dedicated her life to God and taking care of her mother-in-law. In the midst of this, God brought Ruth a husband named Boaz.

The promise God gave me came out of this story. He would bring me a "Boaz," a godly husband. From the time I was divorced up to this time, I did not date at all. I did not go out looking for or seeking a husband. I was going to wait on the Lord to bring me someone. I didn't trust myself to find someone, but I could trust the Lord with that. So that is where I left it.

I would now like to share the history and signs that I received that a Boaz was coming.

The first one came through my mom. The morning that I called her to tell her and my dad I was handing in the paperwork for the divorce. my mom said, "Dianna, I have to tell you something."

I said, "Go ahead, Mom."

She said, "I had a dream about a year ago. In the dream, you were standing there, and all of a sudden, a man I didn't know walked up to you and stood by you. In the dream. I knew he was a very godly man. At the time, I was upset by the dream because I thought you might be cheating on your husband, but I knew you wouldn't do that. I realize now what it was about."

I said, "Mom, why are you telling me now?"

She said, "It is to give you hope."

I trust my mom completely, so I knew she was not making this up. She would never do that. Secondly, her answer about hope I knew was not her words but that of the Holy Spirit. It was out of character for her to answer that way. It did give me hope. I believed God was saying to me I would not be alone in the future. He would bring me another husband.

The next sign came through a dream about two months after I was divorced. I was in the basement of the church that I grew up in. When I walked upstairs, the church was full, and all the people sitting in the church turned and saw me and said, "Shhh, there is a wedding about to start."

I asked, "Who is getting married." I somehow knew it was me, but I would have to wait a long time for this to actually take place.

The second confirmation dream came seven months later. I was standing in my kitchen, and everything that I was seeing was all in white. There was a very small man standing in my kitchen with a spoon, throwing sugar on my countertops. I said, "Stop making a mess!"

He replied, "No, it's really sweet!" He then said, "Do you have any aloe?"

I replied, "Yes, I do." He then took my arm and placed it on his shoulder, and we walked away to get the aloe.

The interpretation of the dream is that a husband is coming. It will be really "sweet"! He has been hurt deeply, but I will bring healing to him. That's what aloe does! The all-white kitchen represents that it will be pure, holy, and redemptive. The very next morning the verse in my devotions was Acts 27:25 (NASB), "Therefore, keep up your courage, men, for I believe God, that it will turn out exactly as I have been told."

Three months later, on the opening day of hunting season, came the next one. I was in my kitchen doing dishes, looking out the window that is above my kitchen sink. My brother-in-law had been in my woods hunting, and he came up to his truck to leave. I watched him get in his truck and shut the door. He began to back up, turn, go forward, back up, turn, go forward and repeated that same scenario several times. I thought, *What is he doing?* I have a very large parking space by the house. There were no other cars parked around him. I just couldn't understand what he was doing. When he finally pulled away, I looked up to see. In the snow on the ground where he had been, I saw two perfect hearts intertwined. As I was looking at them in shock, I felt the Lord remind me of the promise of a Boaz, and it was now written on my land!

I went out and snapped a picture of the hearts because I knew no one would believe me if I told them. I tried and tried to figure out how those hearts were formed, and I couldn't. My brother-in-law did *not* do it on purpose. He was just as shocked as I was when he saw the picture. I knew God had done it.

I would not get another sign until three years later. This one came in the form of another dream. In the dream, I was playing hide-and-seek in a church with the pastor. I was hiding under a pew, waiting for him to find me. My heart was really pumping, and I was so excited to be found!

The interpretation of the dream is that my Boaz would be a preacher! He would be coming to find me.

Throughout the years, as no Boaz would come, I would get discouraged and start to give up that I must have heard wrong. Just as the doubt would start, He would give me another sign. The next one would come through my dad two years later. He and mom were living with me at the time that he had this dream.

In the dream, my dad was walking outside. It was wintertime. He was approaching a church when a big wind came up. He heard in the dream, "Your youngest daughter is getting married today." That was the end of the dream.

When I got up and came downstairs where my dad was sitting, he told me the dream. This one is somewhat self-explanatory. The wind represents the Holy Spirit. I am the youngest daughter he has. The Lord was sending a message to my dad that I would be married again. It would be the Lord's doing as indicated by the strong wind in the dream. I think this meant a lot to my dad because it is very hard for him to see me single and have to work and struggle so hard just to live.

It would be a year and a half before the next sign came. The sign came in the form of two words. No matter where I went, what I did, or what I saw, these two words were in front of me—"new beginning." The Lord even had a chrysalis form on a box in the pole barn. There was no way it should have been there. The chrysalis was for a monarch butterfly. I watched the butterfly come out and quickly assessed it was a female, which I believe was an amazing picture from the Lord of what He had been saying to me—"new beginning."

I googled the process of the caterpillar to chrysalis to butterfly. I was amazed by what I read. When the caterpillar begins to start the process of becoming a chrysalis, he emits a chemical that actually kills himself inside the chrysalis. There are discs that are formed in the caterpillar from birth that once the caterpillar is dead would now come to life to form the butterfly. So in other words, there is nothing left of the caterpillar, and the butterfly is a completely new creature!

The Lord had been working in my heart, mind, body, and soul over the last seven years to get me ready for the new life I was about to begin to step into. None of the old could go into this new place that He was taking me. I felt like I have been in the refining fire and was now ready to come forth as gold fit for the Master's use, ready for whatever He had next for me. He is getting ready to rewrite my story!

This new beginning would be with my Boaz!

My next sign was a dream which I had the night after finding the chrysalis. I was walking along a very dark narrow passageway.

There was a man on my left. He was very close beside me with his arm around my waist. I did not look at him, but I knew it was a man. I was not afraid of him. We were about to step out into an open area that was lit. He pivoted on his right foot and swung his face right in front of mine. He planted a kiss right on my lips. I was shocked and said to him, "Who are you? Where did you come from?" I was not afraid of him.

When I woke up, I had no idea what the dream meant. I did not know who the man was. I had never seen him before. I just kind of blew the dream off because I wasn't sure what to do with it.

Two weeks later, it was the last day of our garage sale that we do once a year for Operation Christmas Child. We (all my OCC volunteers) were waiting on people as they came. A lady came to the sale who was *very* pregnant. When I saw her, I was thinking she was going to have that baby right here right now. She picked up a few things to buy and went to Carolyn, the one taking the money for the day.

Carolyn said to the lady, "Do you know what you are having?"

She said, "Yes, a boy!"

Carolyn then asked her, "Do you have a name picked out?"

She said, "Yes. We are going to name him Boaz, but we will call him Bo."

All of my volunteers were close enough to hear the whole conversation. When we heard "Boaz," our eyes got huge, and we looked at each other and just busted out laughing. All the ladies that are in the sewing group knew about my Boaz story. The lady looked at us like what is your problem.

I said to her, "Oh, ma'am, I am sorry. Let me explain." I told her that I had been waiting seven years for a Boaz to come. She understood and left the sale.

When she left, I said to the Lord, "What was that? What are You saying to me?"

I heard Him say to me, "Boaz is about to be delivered! The promise is about to be fulfilled!"

About the Author

Dianna feels she is very privileged to live in the most beautiful place on the planet, Traverse City, Michigan. It's where cherries, sunny beaches, and sand dunes are at every turn. If she's not at work, then she is engaged with Operation Christmas Child. If there are a few spare moments, then she enjoys nature walks, kayaking down the Platte River, or enjoying a Moomers ice cream cone! Her heart's desire is to see everyone walking in freedom and the call God has on their life. The fields are white and ripe for this everywhere. So her antenna is always up for a divine appointment to engage someone in this way. She feels very blessed to have three of her sons living just a few miles away and the fourth one in Washington State. Her nine host sons are scattered around the world. She has four grandchildren that have stolen her heart. Her life is full and overflowing with His abundant blessings!